I0080983

Opera For People Who Don't Like It

Opera For People Who Don't Like It

Kathy Minicozzi

Published 2015 by HumorOutcasts Press
Printed in the United States of America

ISBN: 0-692-55385-1
EAN-13: 978-069255385-5

Acknowledgments

I want to thank all of the people who taught me how to sing and encouraged me to follow my dream: Chloe Owen; Margaret West Davis, Lois Alexander and Joseph Holloway.

I want to thank Boris Goldovsky, who taught a bunch of us how to move around a stage to music and look realistic at the same time (which is quite a trick).

I want to thank the American Institute of Musical Studies for helping me make the transition to an operatic singing career overseas. I would also like to extend thanks to Tony Amato, Joann Grillo, Richard Kness, Barbara Giancola, Atarah Hazzan and Santa Aronica for believing in me and giving me opportunities.

Thanks to the Undergraduate Creative Writing Department at Columbia University and the Gotham Writers' Workshop in New York City for those wonderful classes, where I finally figured out that yes, I could be a writer if I listened to people who knew what they were talking about and worked hard at it.

Thanks to John Kachuba for teaching me how to write funny and to Donna Cavanagh for giving me ample opportunity to do that. Thanks to all my writing workshop classmates and to my fellow humor writers, especially the ones who take the time to post witty comments to my online posts.

Last but not least, thanks to my friends and family members who have read my attempts to be funny in writing and encouraged me to keep on with it: Michelle Wright, Joan Sullivan, Dorothy Wildhagen, and my nieces Jennifer and Melissa.

If I forgot anyone, I apologize. Many, many people have touched my life and my two chosen arts in very positive ways, and I thank God for all of you.

Opera is where a guy gets stabbed in the back, and instead of dying, he sings.

-- Robert Benchley

INTRODUCTION: Singing Opera and Writing Funny

I am weird, but not dangerous. Okay, maybe I'm dangerous when I'm on a stepladder trying to install a window shade. Other than that, I am harmless and kind of cute, in a way.

But I sing opera and I write funny stuff. Go ahead and look at me like I have two heads. I don't mind. I wish I did have two heads, so I could change them back and forth, according to the look I wanted. But I don't. Have two heads, that is.

Don't ask me to explain in detail how I ended up being an aging opera singer and budding humor writer. It would take too long. Besides, I might write my memoirs someday, and if you already know all about my life you won't want to buy a copy.

My father, who didn't have much faith in the earning power of a singing career, urged me to get an Education degree so that I could become a teacher. The teaching profession is a noble one, and good, dedicated teachers are always needed. That was my problem. I would have been a terrible teacher, and I hated the whole idea. So I got my degrees – B.A. and M.A. – in music, and set out to be an opera singer. Fortunately, I had office skills to fall back on, so I didn't starve in the process, and, although I never sang at the Metropolitan Opera or La Scala or any of the other major houses, I had a much better career singing in smaller places than most of my opera singing colleagues.

The process of building an opera career is difficult, filled with traveling on a shoestring, singing many auditions for every job you get, rejection which is relieved by an occasional encouragement, backstage intrigues, greedy, sometimes unscrupulous agents and colleagues who are either the finest people in the world or the most treacherous (and you have to find out who is which, sometimes the hard way). If you make headway in the business, you also have to deal with spending huge amounts of time away from home. For some of us, this means picking up and making a new home in another country, with another culture and another language. There is also a thing called poverty, caused in good part by the big expenses involved in a singing career: voice lessons; coachings; audition wardrobe; printed music; mailings; travel all over the place; etc.

When you get onstage, though, and you are in good voice and the performance is going well, it's the most satisfying, practically orgasmic thing in the world.

Now that I am a woman of a certain age, no longer actively pursuing an international singing career, you would think I would settle down, get a job with benefits, look for some lucrative sidelines to build up something for my old age, and reflect back on all the fun I had. I actually did one of those things. I got a job with benefits, at which I work five days a week. Instead of lucrative sidelines, I chose to become a writer. I guess I can't live without dedicating huge amounts of time and energy to something at which most practitioners never make any money.

The process of building a writing career is difficult, filled with things like submitting work to many publishers for every acceptance you get, rejection which is relieved by an occasional encouragement, greedy vanity publishers and other people dying to take a writer's money, and colleagues who are either the most supportive people in the world or the most envious (and you have to find out who is which, sometimes the hard way). If you hope to be able to live only on your writing without any other source of income, you also have the prospect of poverty.

This is a clear case of *déjà vu.* I have gone from one profession where the prospects of getting rich are dismal and the rejection is constant to another profession where the prospects of getting rich are dismal and the rejection is constant. What can I say?

I'll say this: writing is hard work, but it's fun. Like singing, it is satisfying in a visceral way. It is even more satisfying to me if I can make people laugh. I can't imagine a life without doing something that I love to do, so this is it.

The irony, which I think is hilarious, is that, in other ways, singing opera is the direct opposite of writing humor. I have listed the disparities below.

SINGING OPERA vs. WRITING FUNNY

Opera: I have played serious, tragic, beautiful heroines. I have died onstage of everything from tuberculosis to poison to hara-kiri to jumping off a building, while costumed in gorgeous gowns, peasant costumes, a poor seamstress' dress, kimonos and nightgowns. I have worn glamorous wigs and complicated hairdos and my face has been covered with a thick layer of gooey stage makeup.

Writing: I often sit in front of my computer looking like a bag lady in the most comfortable things I have that are clean. Sometimes I just leave my PJs on. Nobody is looking at me, so what the hell. If by some chance anyone *is* looking at me, I'm covered up and that's what matters. I never wear makeup if I can help it. And I have not died yet, at least not that I know of.

Opera: I am in front of a bunch of people, singing very loudly and hoping for a lot of applause.

Writing: I am in front of my cat, typing on a computer keyboard and hoping to get a few laughs. If I sing I scare the cat.

Opera: People have sometimes asked me to sing something on the spur of the moment, especially at parties or family get-togethers. On the other hand, if I break out in spontaneous song in public, the people I am with pretend they don't know me.

Writing: Nobody ever asks me for a free writing sample, and I have to practically bribe my family members to read my stuff. I can sit in a public place, such as a café or a park, and write until my fingers get tired without attracting any attention at all.

Opera: Opera singers try to avoid getting sick, especially with performances coming up, even if it means putting themselves in an isolation booth.

Writing: I don't want to get sick, but if I don't get out and around (breathing germs and touching things like subway poles and escalator rails) I won't find anything funny to write about. Agoraphobia jokes get old really fast. Writers are expected to be observers and interactors. It comes with the vocation.

That's enough. You get the picture.

What is the one subject that an opera singer turned humor writer should write about? Opera, of course! Opera is one of the greatest art forms ever invented. It is a marriage of great music and drama. It can move audiences in a special way not shared with other forms of theater. Operagoers easily become hooked, because they love it.

It is also rich in possibilities for humor. That's where I come in. Just because I love opera and even sing it doesn't mean I can't poke fun at it.

By the way, as a humor writer I am allowed to exaggerate to make something funny. Please remember that when you read this book. Opera is one of the greatest, most fascinating art forms ever developed and perfected by humans. Attending a good performance is an incredible, cathartic experience. *Singing* a good performance can be just as cathartic in another way. If I appear to be dissing opera in this book, know that that is the farthest thing from my mind. What I do here is like cracking jokes at a good friend who is free to crack jokes right back. In a way, I am also poking fun of myself.

I hope that, by now, you have been so captivated by my brilliant lead-in that you just HAVE to stick around and read the rest of this book.

CHAPTER 1: HONK IF YOU DON'T LIKE OPERA

It has come to my attention that there are people who don't like opera. My opinion is that we all have a right to dislike whatever we feel like disliking because we have free will, opposable thumbs and brains designed for higher thought. However, I have spent a great part of my lifetime singing opera, and I think that attending an opera is an experience worth trying at least once, because, like crack cocaine, it can become addictive once you have been exposed to it. Unlike crack cocaine, though, opera is a harmless, if sometimes expensive, habit.

As an introduction, here are a few synopses of the stories of some well-known operas, told in a way that we can all understand.

CARMEN

Composer: Georges Bizet

Language: French, even though it takes place in Spain[1]

A psychopath with a bad temper falls madly in love with a whore, who gets sick of him fast. The psycho has to go home for a while to take care of some family business. The whore takes the opportunity to dump him and take up with a bullfighter. The psycho comes back and finds her. They have a big fight and he kills her, after which he is very sorry.

---

[1] That's nothing. Puccini's *Turandot*, which is sung in Italian, takes place in China. At least France and Spain border each other, so it's not quite such a stretch.

LA TRAVIATA

Composer: Giuseppe Verdi

Language: Italian, even though it takes place in France

A rash young guy with a temper falls in love with a high-class prostitute. (Do you see a pattern here?) This time the prostitute falls in love right back. They set up house together out in the country. The rash young guy's bourgeois father comes around and persuades the prostitute that it would be in everybody's best interest if she would break up with his son, because it is embarrassing to have a prostitute in the family, even if she and the son are only living together. It kills her to give him up, but she does. The son is very unhappy, and takes it out on her. In the last act, she dies of tuberculosis and everyone is sorry they treated her so badly.

If this story looks familiar, it's because it is. It is based on *La Dame aux Camélias* by Alexandre Dumas Fils, which, in turn, inspired the movie *Camille*. If you like really old movies, you'll know this one. Hint: it stars Greta Garbo, if that helps. No, I am not old enough to remember that movie. I saw it on cable TV.

LA BOHÈME

Composer: Giacomo Puccini

Language: Italian. You guessed it. It takes place in Paris, France.[2]

Four starving young artist types are sharing a one-room attic apartment in Paris. To say the place is a dump is to compliment it. One of them, a dreamy poet, falls in love with an equally dreamy seamstress who lives in an equally squalid room in the same rat hole. Of course, there is also another couple, a painter and his sometime hooker girlfriend. Hookers are something of an operatic tradition, as you have noticed.

Both couples break up, but that's only Act III. There is one more act to go. It turns out that the dreamy young seamstress has – yes, that's right – tuberculosis! In true operatic fashion, she dies of it, right after reconnecting with the dreamy young poet. This is the end of the opera, because it would be pointless to go on after that.

[2] Believe it or not, some Italian operas take place in Italy.

DON GIOVANNI

Composer: Wolfgang Amadeus Mozart

Language: Italian, even though the composer was an Austrian and it takes place in Spain

Don Giovanni, a/k/a Don Juan, chases every woman who comes within his orbit – well, two women, anyway. The opera takes place within a short period. In addition, he gets sidetracked by fighting and killing an elderly man in Act 1, then running into one of his old conquests, who still has the flaming hots for him, stalks him and steps in and interferes whenever he is about to make headway with another woman. He doesn't get lucky even once, and is dragged down to hell by demons after he refuses to repent and change his ways because (1) he's been having too much fun and doesn't want to stop and (2) he's stupid. The order for him to repent comes from the statue of the elderly man he kills in Act 1. Don't ask.

I PAGLIACCI

Composer: Ruggiero Leoncavallo

Language: Italian, and it takes place in Italy this time

A scruffy troop of traveling *Commedia dell' Arte* players arrives in a village somewhere in Calabria, Italy to give a performance. It's a Mom and Pop operation; the leading man is married to the leading lady. The leading lady can't stand him, though, and she plans to run away with her boyfriend, who lives in the village. One of the other actors, who has the hots for the wife and is sore because she thinks he's repulsive,[3] tells her husband about the way his wife has been putting the horns on his head. The husband stabs the wife and her boyfriend to death during the performance, at which point the performance is over, with no refunds.

[3] She emphasizes this message by hitting him with a whip. No, it isn't THAT kind of whip. Get your minds out of the gutter!

FAUST

Composer: Charles Gounod

Language: French, although it takes place in Germany

A bored old scholar gives his soul to the Devil and is made young again. He meets a pretty girl at a fair and seduces her. She gets knocked up, has a baby, goes crazy, kills the baby and ends up condemned to death. Faust and the Devil plot to spring her from jail, but instead of being sprung she repents and goes to Heaven. The Devil is left frustrated and Faust is left looking like an idiot and wondering what just happened.

So, you see, opera is not so painful after all.

If you are attending a performance produced by a small, local opera company trying to work with almost no money, you are likely to be presented with minimal scenery that doesn't correspond to the time period in which the opera takes place, costumes that the singers found in local thrift shops and costume jewelry that is definitely NOT of the family heirloom type. The singers will try their best to make their hair look authentic, using whatever they have, and most of them do a fair job of it.

The "orchestra" in these performances is usually a piano.

The great thing about attending such a performance is that it is almost always in a small space, close and personal, and the singers are often accessible after the performance, if you want to compliment them, start a conversation and/or get an autograph on your program.

If you are attending a performance in a major opera house you are going to be treated to a grand spectacle, with often well-known singers and beautiful scenery and costumes. The beauty of the production sometimes lessens the pain when the staging is ridiculous or the singing is sub-par. Only veteran operagoers are likely to concern themselves with those things, though. Beginners are free to enjoy the scenery, and even to applaud it, although the opera cognoscenti in the audience will consider that a sign of a real dilettante.

What I am getting at, in too many words, is that there is always something to enjoy in an opera production.

CHAPTER 2: THE STORIES

Opera is more than just funny-looking, middle-aged fat people in period costumes making loud, funny sounds and ridiculous gestures. An opera is a play, with a plot. The only differences between operas and spoken plays are: (1) operas are sung (d'oh!); and (2) they are usually sung in Italian, German, French, Russian, Czech or whatever other language they were written in. More operas were written in Italian than any other language. The Italians started the whole thing to begin with, and Italians are natural show-offs who love beautiful singing and emotional displays. The Germans tried to catch up, but they never quite made it. Their excuse was that they preferred quality to quantity. Actually, they were just being snobs.

Yes, there are some operas written in English. British and American composers popped up all over the place during the 20th Century, and they figured it would be silly to write operas in Italian or German when they had a perfectly good language of their own. Some of these operas are good; performances pop up now and then in the smaller, regional houses and singers excerpt arias from them for auditions. Many a soprano has sung "Ain't It a Pretty Night" from Carlisle Floyd's *Susannah,* and many a mezzo-soprano has shown how she can suffer with "Must the Winter Come So Soon?" from Samuel Barber's *Vanessa.*

I know what you're thinking: "Yes, give us operas in English, so we can understand what the hell is going on!" Think again. The diction of most opera singers is so bad that they might as well be singing in Tasmanian. They are more concerned with clear, ringing tones than clear, ringing words. This leaves beginner operagoers right where they began – not knowing what the hell is going on.

Opera companies finally decided to do their audiences a favor and project titles above the stage. All of a sudden, people knew what was happening onstage and what the characters were singing. They were even laughing at the funny parts (and sometimes at bad translations). In a supreme act of one-upmanship, New York's Metropolitan Opera put *their* titles on the backs of the seats and gave each audience member the option to figure out how to turn them on in the dark.

What does all that have to do with the stories of the operas? Not much. I just thought I'd throw it in, for the hell of it. It increases my word count.

Now that I got that out of the way, I'll get to the point.

What's the subject again? Oh yes – plots.

People think that opera is a high-classed art form, fit only for polite, pretentious society where people drink tea out of fancy porcelain cups and everybody has a lot of money to throw away to make themselves look better than they really do. WRONG! Opera plots are full of things like intrigue, seduction, murder, suicide, incest, betrayal, attempted rape, grand larceny, deception, terminal disease, curses, ghosts and demons, all covered in a veneer of music. It's as if the producers of the ID Channel decided to adapt their shows to the Hallmark Channel. You just can't disguise ID Channel material, no matter how hard you try. As the great Anna Russell once said in her hilarious "analysis" of *Der Ring des Nibelungen* by Richard Wagner, "That's the beauty of grand opera. You can do anything, so long as you sing it!" (If you're wondering what *Der Ring des Nibelungen* is and who the hell Richard Wagner was, I'll explain all that in a later chapter.) In other words, the stuff of opera is not the stuff most parents want their kids to watch on TV.

Example: Giuseppe Verdi's *Rigoletto*

If you take a good look at the *libretto* (i.e. "book") of this opera, you notice that almost all of the characters are repulsive. The only exception is the leading soprano, and she's disgustingly naïve. Nobody's perfect, but these people are ridiculous.[4]

Rigoletto is a jester at the court of the Duke of Mantua, sometime during the Italian Renaissance. The Duke is a douchebag who is slowly making his way through all the good-looking women in his immediate geographical area, including the wife of one of his own courtiers and sycophants. ("Sex is like a buffet and I'm hungry!" he

---

[4] This opera is based on a play by the French author Victor Hugo, who also gave us *Les Miserables* and *The Hunchback of Notre Dame*. That's no excuse for Verdi, but it's an interesting bit of trivia, if you're into that kind of thing.

proclaims, paying no attention to the husband, who is hyperventilating nearby.) His excuse is that all women are unfaithful, anyway, so he might as well beat them to it and have some fun in the process. He's married, by the way, although his wife never appears in the opera; she is only mentioned briefly, once, in Act II.

Rigoletto is a Don Rickles type of court jester, who insults everybody for a laugh (except the Duke, naturally. Rigoletto isn't stupid.) Everybody hates him. In addition to that, he's a hunchback, which affects his self-esteem in a negative way. He loves his daughter Gilda, the disgustingly naïve one. She can't help being disgustingly naïve, though. Rigoletto has deliberately sheltered her all her life, which has not been very long, because she's pretty young. Rigoletto wants to save her from falling for the wrong guy, among other things. We soon see how that goes.

Unknown to everyone else, the Duke has had his eye on a new girl in town, who turns out to be – of all people – Gilda! The Duke's courtiers, who are sick of all of Rigoletto's nasty jibes, kidnap Gilda right under Rigoletto's nose and bring her to the palace. We don't see what happens backstage, whether it's consensual or not, but when Gilda comes out of the Duke's apartments she is more experienced than she was when she went in. Rigoletto, of course, is mad as hell and determined to take revenge on the Duke.

Gilda ends up falling madly in love with the Duke, which makes things even more complicated for Rigoletto, as if he doesn't have enough problems. He hires a professional hit man named Sparafucile to kill the Duke.[5] Sparafucile

[5] There was no Mafia during the Renaissance, but there was a decent amount of work for an experienced freelance assassin.

owns a dive on the edge of town where a guy can get some good cheap wine and follow it up with Sparafucile's sexy sister Maddalena. The Duke is lured out to Casa Sparafucile. Rigoletto turns up, too, dragging Gilda along so they can spy on the Duke through a hole in the wall. Why there is a hole in Sparafucile's wall, we are never told. My guess is that he failed to pay his last repairman and the job was left half-done. The repairman was probably killed, just to teach him a lesson, and buried under the wall somewhere. Don't pay any attention to me on this subject. I watch too many episodes of *Mobsters* on cable TV.

To get back to the story, Gilda sees the Duke trying to grope Maddalena, and gets very disturbed. She and her Dad go away, but Gilda sneaks back, overhears Sparafucile and Maddalena, with Maddalena pleading that SHE loves the Duke,[6] so would her brother please not kill him, but kill someone else instead, like Rigoletto. Sparafucile, being an honorable assassin, is reluctant to kill a client. He doesn't have enough customers yet to be able to afford to lose one of them. Because he knows he'll never hear the end of it if he doesn't go along with Maddalena, Sparafucile agrees to kill the next person who comes to the inn and pass him off as the Duke. In a fit of self-sacrifice, Gilda knocks on the door and they let her in.

A little later, Rigoletto comes to pay Sparafucile the other half of his fee (having paid half in advance) and collect what he thinks will be the body of the Duke, stuffed in a

[6] I guess nobody told Maddalena that loving the Duke means she'll have to take a number.

sack, ready to be thrown into the river. When he finds Gilda in the sack instead, he goes crazy. By some miracle, Gilda is still alive enough to sing a final, tear-jerking duet before she dies.[7] What happens to Rigoletto after that, we never find out.

Some famous excerpts from this opera include:

Aria: *Questa o quella*, sung by the Duke

Aria: *Caro nome*, sung by Gilda

Aria: *Cortiggiani, vil razza dannata*, sung by Rigoletto

Aria: *La donna è mobile*, sung by the Duke (tenors get more than their share of the glory)

Quartet: *Bella figlia dell' amore*, sung by the Duke, Maddalena, Gilda and Rigoletto

Although most operas have tragic plots, there *are* comic operas. These are the ones that are funny on purpose, and not just because of stupid staging or bad acting. The advent of supertitles has made it possible for audiences to get the jokes, and the result has been laughter in all the right places, where previously there was only reverential silence. In other words, people are having more fun.

Example: Gioacchino Rossini's *The Barber of Seville*

The young Count Almaviva is in love with a girl named Rosina and he wants to get to know her better and marry her. Rosina has the same ideas about the count. You'd think that

[7] Sparafucile needs a lot of practice with his stabbing technique. He is probably just an apprentice assassin, working for his license.

would make their marriage a done deal, right? Think again. Rosina is the ward (read "prisoner with room and board") of a greedy, elderly physician, Dr. Bartolo. Dr. Bartolo wants to marry Rosina and take over her money, of which she has scads and scads. She's the 18th Century version of a trust fund kid. The problem is the idea of marrying Bartolo makes Rosina want to vomit. To help him get Rosina's consent, Dr. Bartolo asks help from a friend, Don Basilio, a music teacher, who is just as nasty and devious as he is, but a lot smarter. Basilio's job, besides giving singing lessons to Rosina, is to give Bartolo some good, sneaky ideas and help him carry them through.

The opera begins with Count Almaviva singing an early morning serenade under Rosina's balcony. She doesn't appear, but the person who does appear, on his way to work, is Figaro the barber, who just happens to be an old acquaintance of the count. Figaro gets a grand entrance, singing one of the most famous baritone arias ever written, *Largo al factotum,* or *Out of the Way, Here I Come.* In case there might be some people listening who don't know who he is, he repeats his name over and over. It's a cheap way of advertising.

Count Almaviva can't believe his luck. Not only is Figaro smart, he is even better at outwitting everyone than Don Basilio, who has won lifetime recognition as National Deviousness Champion of Spain. In addition, Figaro knows Dr. Bartolo's household very well, because he is Bartolo's barber, wig stylist and whatever else Bartolo will pay him to do. Figaro agrees to help the count, for a financial consideration (of course), and he gets the count to sing another serenade. Calling himself "Lindoro," Almaviva sings that he is not rich (which is a lie, because he is), but that he gives Rosina his heart and his loving, faithful soul. This time Rosina answers him, only to be startled by something inside the house and pull away from the window. The count is upset, but Figaro gives him a couple of good ideas to get him started on a plan to rescue Rosina from Bartolo's house and marry her himself. The count, who has more looks, charm and money than brains, needs all the help he can get.

In the meantime, Rosina, who is as smart as Figaro and determined to get out of Bartolo's house and into "Lindoro's," is doing some plotting on her own. So are Bartolo and Basilio. Basilio wants Bartolo to start some juicy gossip about the count, but Bartolo says no, he's in too much of a hurry to start writing for People Magazine; he wants to drag Rosina to the altar ASAP and start spending her money. Figaro overhears this and joins forces with Rosina. Figaro has already set up the fake Lindoro to come in pretending to be a drunken soldier, with orders saying he is to be quartered in Bartolo's house. (People had to do that in those days; it was a big pain in the tush.) Count Almaviva makes his pretend-drunk entrance with a lot of noise, staggering and mispronouncing of Bartolo's name. Bartolo comes up with a legal document stating that he is exempt from quartering soldiers in his house, drunk or sober. Almaviva refuses to go away, and a big brouhaha results, with the police showing up, everybody getting discombobulated and the whole plan going awry.

That isn't the end of it, though. Almaviva/Lindoro makes another entry into the house, this time disguised as a music teacher, come to give Rosina a singing lesson. He tells Bartolo that Basilio is sick, and has sent him instead. Rosina sings to Almaviva's accompaniment, while Bartolo, who is nosy and controlling, sits in on the lesson. Figaro comes in, claiming that it is his day to come and shave Bartolo. Unexpectedly, Don Basilio comes in. Almaviva, Rosina and Figaro tell him that he is terribly sick and, with a monetary bribe, convince him to go home. While Figaro is shaving Bartolo, Rosina and her "Lindoro" pretend to be talking about the music she has just sung, while, of course, they are talking over plans for her escape. At one point, they forget themselves and talk too loud, Bartolo hears them and, again, "Lindoro" and Figaro have to get out fast.

Bartolo gets Basilio to come, bringing a notary, so he can marry Rosina fast, before the count gets in again. They show Rosina a letter that she had written to "Lindoro," telling her that it had been used in a nefarious plot by "Lindoro" to give her, Rosina, to the evil Count Almaviva! Rosina is heartbroken, and damned mad, and makes a stupid decision to marry Bartolo on the rebound. Everybody goes off to get ready for a wedding. Figaro and Almaviva sneak in, using a key that Figaro had stolen earlier. Rosina confronts "Lindoro." "Lindoro" reveals himself as having been Almaviva all along. Rosina is relieved, and feels really stupid and sorry. Basilio comes in with the notary. He is offered a bribe, the count points a gun at him just to show he's serious, and Basilio agrees to witness the marriage of Almaviva and Rosina. Bartolo comes in too late and is forced to admit defeat. Everyone is happy except Bartolo, who is hopping mad about losing Rosina's money, and Basilio, who doesn't care, as long as he gets paid by somebody or other.

Some well-known excerpts from this opera are:

Aria: *Ecco ridente in cielo*, sung by Count Almaviva

Aria: *Largo al factotum*, sung by Figaro

Aria: *Una voce poco fa*, sung by Rosina. If the singer is a mezzo-soprano, this aria is sung in the original key. If she's a soprano, she transposes it up. Hopefully, the orchestra has the right version.

Duet: *Dunque io son*, sung by Rosina and Figaro

Aria: *La calunnia*, sung by Don Basilio

Aria: *A un dottor della mia sorte*, sung by Dr. Bartolo

Pretty sharp, huh?

CHAPTER 3: MODERN PRODUCTIONS

There was a time in the history of opera when singers ruled. If you had a great voice, it wouldn't matter if you looked like a gorilla. You were in. Stage directors would never dare to ask you to do something you didn't want to do, and if you were famous enough you could even skip rehearsals without being canned. Your conception of the role you were playing (if you actually had a conception) overruled everyone else's. The great tenor Lauritz Melchior, who probably sang more performances of the roles of Tristan and Siegfried than all of his stage directors put together had years in their lives, once remarked that if he thought anyone had anything to teach him they could make an appointment and meet him in his apartment. Audiences loved Mr. Melchior, and he is still considered one of the great singers of the 20th Century, so he must have been doing something right.

This was known as The Golden Age.

In the meantime, stage directors were hiding in the wings, in the curtain, in the orchestra pit behind the brass section and in the men's room, just waiting for their opportunity to stage a coup. And they did. Big time. And once they came into power, it went right to their heads. BIG time.

Would you like to know what kind of mind-erasing craziness operatic stage directors have been foisting on the world? I'll tell you, anyway.

Let's say, hypothetically, that there is a company called The City Island Opera Company, they are doing a production of Verdi's *Aïda* and the Board of Directors is trying to decide who to hire as stage director. They narrow it down to Director A and Director B.

Director A is very traditional. He puts the story where Verdi put it, in ancient Egypt. It's a tragic love triangle between Aïda, a sweet, loving Ethiopian slave who is actually the daughter of the King of Ethiopia, although nobody knows this; Radames, a hot, ambitious, macho Egyptian general; and Amneris, the smart, devious, bitchy, spoiled daughter of the current Pharaoh.

It's an uneven contest, because Amneris is an alpha female who has the advantage of being smarter than everyone within a ten-mile radius. Aïda's only advantages are that she's hot, she's sweet and she is good at keeping a secret. Both women are capable of being sneaky and manipulative, although it comes naturally to Amneris, whereas Aïda has to work at it, and she's no match for the other woman. If Amneris were alive today, she would make a fabulous police interrogator. She can get into someone's head faster than an idea.

Aïda being secretly the daughter of the Ethiopian king causes all kinds of complications and gets Radames in a mess of trouble, because Egypt is at war with Ethiopia at the time and it is considered bad form for a general to consort with the enemy, especially when Amneris catches him getting ready to abscond with Aïda the night before he's due to marry Amneris. To Radames' credit, he has been trapped into those marriage plans against his will. Only someone who doesn't know Amneris would consider that a good excuse, because she doesn't take no for an answer and she's capable of some ingenious revenge. As you can imagine, the fact that he was trapped into being part of Amneris' wedding plans doesn't help Radames, especially when he tells Amneris, to her face, to shove it where the sun doesn't shine, in a very dramatic scene just before he is taken to face a kangaroo court full of the same people who had been promoting him earlier, but who were now embarrassed and damn mad and ready to shove him into a tomb ASAP. They don't even take the time to kill him first. They find some unused ancient Egyptian tomb and shove him into it alive. Aïda, who somehow knows just where Radames is going to wind up, is already there, waiting to die with him, which everyone in the audience thinks is *so* romantic. The scenery is filled with ancient temples and palm trees along the Nile and everyone is dressed like a painting on an old scrap of papyrus.

Director B doesn't want to hear about tradition. Tradition gives him the hives. He places the opera on a huge spaceship loaded with bananas, headed for a planet that the people on board plan to conquer and colonize after turning the inhabitants into banana plants. Aïda is one of those inhabitants. How she got on board the spaceship is never explained, but she's a prisoner and a slave and, secretly, the daughter of the king of the prospective banana people. Instead of being Ethiopian, she's a purple-skinned space alien. Radames is the captain of the spaceship. Amneris is the daughter of the evil emperor of the planet that is sending the bananas and the space army.

The bananas that cover the stage are supposed to represent something, although what they represent is anybody's guess. The director claims that they represent the invasion of virgin territory by alien species. Most of the audience thinks they just represent the fruitiness of the whole production. Some people with dirtier minds think the bananas represent rampant phallic sex. The performers have all they can do to keep from stepping on the bananas and falling down. The director refuses to use fake bananas because he wants "realism."

In the end, it is Amneris who dies with Radames, while Aïda's voice is heard as a disembodied spirit because she has prematurely turned herself into a purple-skinned alien banana. Amneris and Radames are not buried alive; they are jettisoned out into space, along with a bag full of shredded paper and a few banana peels. All the men in the cast wear plain, red uniforms and all the women wear silver lamé bikinis, even the fat ones.

All references to Egypt, Ethiopia, ancient Egyptian gods and goddesses and the Nile River are left in the text. Those things are irrelevant to the director. The only thing that matters to him is the point he is trying to make about human alienation (or is it invasion, or invasion causing alienation, or what the hell is this guy trying to prove?). Nobody would ever figure out the connection between a spaceship loaded with bananas and human alienation (or whatever), so he has published a long explanation, full of academic language and big words, in the program notes, which few people have the patience or the mindset to read all the way through.

The one thing that everybody knows about this director is that it doesn't bother him to be ridiculous in public.

To strengthen his point of view, Director B has published his explanation in several Ivy League university publications. Everybody there thinks he's a genius, probably because most of them have never had to sit through the staged results of one of his concepts.

The company hires Director B because his concept is innovative and it will make all of them look very intellectual to a couple of snobs among the wealthy donors. Like many snobs, they don't know squat about what they are supporting, but they like to see their names in the program and have everyone think they are smart and cultured.

You see what we are all up against?

At the Metropolitan Opera, Verdi's *Rigoletto* no longer takes place in Renaissance Italy. It has been moved to 1970s Las Vegas. This works surprisingly well, except for the titles on the backs of the seats. The "translations" in the titles read like the script of a gangster movie. You almost expect Sparafucile to come out with, "Salutate il mio piccolo amico"[8] when he stabs Gilda! (Don't worry. He doesn't.) It's kind of fun, in a way. In the middle of a tragic opera, those titles can give the audience some good laughs.

Let us now have a moment of silence to mourn the passing of intelligence and good sense.

8 "Say hello to my little friend!" You all know it's from the movie *Scarface*, released in 1983, directed by Brian de Palma, screenplay by Oliver Stone, starring Al Pacino and Michelle Pfeiffer. There. I gave the right credit!

CHAPTER 4: DEATH, OPERATIC STYLE

In most operas, somebody dies. Usually it's the hero or the heroine, or both of them. Occasionally, someone else will get in on the act, too, not wanting to be left out of all the fun and attention. Whatever or whoever, death in most operas is as inevitable as a tenor's expanding waistline.

Operatic characters don't die like everyone else. For one thing, they die singing. I don't know about the rest of you, but if I were dying of some awful disease or someone had just stabbed or poisoned me, the last thing I would want to do would be to sing about it. "Help! Somebody call 911!" would be my most likely reaction, provided, of course, that I were capable of making any sound at all. Most likely, I'd just fall back and die and leave the commentary to someone else.

In Act I of Mozart's *Don Giovanni,* Don Giovanni (Italian for Don Juan – same guy, different language) has just broken into the bedroom of an attractive woman, with the idea of breaking into *her*. She isn't about to take that lying down, and she makes enough noise to wake up everyone, including her elderly father, while running after Giovanni to keep him from escaping. Donna Anna is hysterical, and one of the dumbest broads in all of opera. This is a dangerous combination. The elderly father and Giovanni get into a sword fight, which lasts about ten seconds until Giovanni runs him through. It isn't a fair fight, but Giovanni is a poor sportsman, in addition to being a real rat bastard.

You'd think that would be the end of the elderly man, but it isn't. Damned if he, Giovanni and Giovanni's servant don't spend the next minute or so singing a trio about how the old man's soul is slowly leaving his "palpitating bosom." It's only on the final cadence of the trio that the old man is finally able to die and be done with it. The poor man gets no rest even then, though. Toward the end of the opera, he comes back as his own statue, just to scare the life out of Giovanni. He succeeds.

Giovanni gets an unusual demise, too. While he's singing about how terrified he is, Hell opens up, with fire, smoke and demons who are trying to out-sing him. The demons win the contest, and with one last scream Giovanni goes right to eternal damnation. There is no soul leaving a palpitating bosom for him. One minute he's up here and the next minute he's down there. Then everybody who is still alive comes onstage and they all sing about how that's the way nasty people end up, just in case the audience didn't already get the message.

Sacrificing yourself for love is another popular operatic death. In a previous chapter, I mentioned Rigoletto's daughter Gilda, who turns herself over to be assassinated in place of the jackass she's in love with. The guy who does the deed is supposedly a professional hit man, but you'd never know it because he can't seem to aim his knife correctly. Gilda lives long enough to be picked up by her father and to sing at least a five-minute duet with him, about how she's going to pray for him up in heaven, as if that would make Rigoletto feel any better about the whole thing.

Speaking of not dying right away, the champion here has to be Desdemona in Verdi's *Otello*. (Those of you who know the Shakespeare play can skip this paragraph because you already know what I'm going to say.) Desdemona is strangled by Otello, who thinks she's dead because she isn't moving, but she isn't dead – yet. Everyone is surprised a minute later when she starts to sing again. She sings a few disjointed sentences about how she's innocent and Otello didn't kill her so nobody should blame him, *then* she dies.

In another Verdi opera, *Il Trovatore*, the heroine, Leonora, also sacrifices herself for love of the tenor, but she doesn't depend on someone else to do it. She takes poison. Unfortunately, it's a quicker acting poison than she thought, her whole plan to save her soul mate gets messed up because the timing is off, and he ends up being beheaded (offstage, fortunately). At least he gets a quick death.

Speaking of suicide, the stupidest example of this has to be the hero of Verdi's *Ernani*, who offs himself just because he promised someone else he would do so and, damn it, he's a man of his word. He was hoping the other guy wouldn't remember his promise, or would just forget about the whole thing, but the other guy is a mean old, conniving bastard and he holds Ernani to his idiotic promise. And they say sopranos are dumb!

In Verdi's *Aïda*, the tenor hero and the soprano heroine end up being sealed alive in a tomb, with no food or water or fresh air, waiting to be found by archaeologists a few thousand years later. That's what you get for living in ancient Egypt and pissing off the Pharaoh's daughter.

Tosca throws herself off the wall of a major tourist attraction in Rome after killing the baritone, who has just had the tenor killed more or less posthumously. Don't ask. Madama Butterfly commits *hara kiri*. In Wagner's *Die Götterdämmerung,* Brunhilde sings for twenty minutes, after which she's tired, so she walks right into a funeral pyre, bringing her horse with her. The fire spreads all over the place, killing just about everybody. Wagner never did like being outdone.

Knives, pistols, poison, swords, terminal illness, magic, fire, bare hands … all are used to great effect in dispatching operatic characters.

CHAPTER 5: THOSE CRAZY GERMANS

In an earlier lesson, I mentioned opera plots and how they are reminiscent of lurid cable TV channels that specialize in re-enacted crimes. As an example, I gave the plot of Verdi's *Rigoletto,* which is a blood and guts Italian opera, complete with love, sex, murder and show-stopping high notes at the end of melodious arias.

Well, the Italians weren't the only ones who liked to set a steamy story to music. The Germans got into the act, too, in a huge way. As everyone from Roman times on has known, it takes a lot to stop the Germans once they set their minds to something, whether it's composing operas, building automobiles or invading their neighbors.

The Germans went the Italians one better. They didn't just have revolting characters and dastardly deeds, they threw in occasional mysticism, mythology and folklore just to make things interesting. Mozart's *The Magic Flute* is full of Masonic symbolism.[9] Humperdinck's *Hansel and Gretel* is the familiar fairy tale with the cannibal witch who ends up being baked in her own oven, which serves her right. Weber's *Der Freischutz* is about trafficking with evil spirits and making magic bullets. If it was weird, some German would set it to music.

The most famous of German opera composers is Richard Wagner. Wagner could have written an opera about his own life. He was a first-class narcissist, besides being an anti-semite and an adulterer.[10] He owed money to everybody, he got in trouble because of his political views, he moved around a lot and he finally settled down in the town of Bayreuth in Bavaria.[11] He figured nobody would take the trouble to go looking for him in that little backwater place, not realizing that, by moving there, he was turning that backwater place into an international tourist attraction. He designed and built a theater in Bayreuth to produce his operas and nobody else's, because he didn't think any other composer was as important as he was. It was *his* theater, and nobody else could have it. Other composers should go get their own theaters. He didn't care, because he never paid them any attention, anyway. The theater was an acoustic masterpiece, and Wagner was not about to share it. Why

---

[9] Yes, I know. Mozart wasn't German. He was Austrian. Who cares? I'm trying to make a point here. Work with me on this.

[10] Old German proverb: The sex is always better in the other man's bedroom.

[11] Not to be confused with Beirut. Please don't go to Beirut looking for Wagner operas. You will only find a lot of Lebanese people who will think you have babaganoush for brains.

nobody else has thought to copy the acoustics of Wagner's theater is one of the music world's great mysteries.

Wagner wrote his own libretti, too. He liked the sound of his own words. He would never say something in two words if he could use fifty. As a result, his operas are l-o-n-g. *Das Ring der Nibelungen* is so long that he had to turn it into FOUR operas instead of just one. Verdi would never have done that. Instead, he would have driven his librettist to drink with constant demands that this, that or the other be changed, added or deleted to make a nice, concise show full of great theatrical timing, dramatic climaxes and loads of emotion. Of course, Verdi was Italian, not German. That explains everything.

Wagner not only wrote his own libretti, he made up a lot of words. Even Germans have trouble understanding the language Wagner came up with. He took the German language and turned it into Wagnerdeutsch. No, there is no such word, even in German. If Wagner could invent words, so can I.

It would take too long to give you what goes on in the *Ring* cycle in detail, but here is a short list of crimes, misdemeanors and other happenings in the four-night event:

1. Alberich the Dwarf renounces love, steals a hunk of magic gold from three brainless floozies who swim around inside the Rhine and forges himself a magic ring to make himself Master of the Universe. – GRAND LARCENY, MEGALOMANIA

2. Wotan, the chief of the gods, builds a huge mansion in the clouds called Valhalla and has trouble paying his contractors, the giants Fasolt and Fafner. – RENEGING ON A DEBT

3. Wotan goes down to where Alberich lives and steals the magic ring and a magic helmet that goes with it. Alberich puts a curse on the ring. – BURGLARY, CRIMINAL ENDANGERMENT

4. Wotan has to give up the magic ring to his two contractors to fulfill the debt and Fafner kills Fasolt for it. – MURDER

5. Wotan just *has* to get that ring back so that he, the Handsome, Sexy Good Guy, can be Master of the Universe instead of those sleazy dwarfs and giants that nobody likes because they're ugly and they have terrible table manners. He goes down to earth and takes up with a mortal woman, in spite of the fact that he is already married to one of the goddesses, Fricka. He and the mortal woman have a couple of mortal kids named Siegmund and Sieglinde. Wotan hopes to train his progeny to help him get his ring back. – ADULTERY AND BIGAMY

6. Siegmund and Sieglinde are separated in childhood, but when they meet again sparks fly, they have an intense affair and Sieglinde gets knocked up. Did I mention that Sieglinde is married to a nasty idiot named Hunding and she can't stand him. – ADULTERY AND INCEST

7. Sieglinde's husband Hunding kills Siegmund and Wotan gets mad and kills Hunding because he has killed his son Siegmund. – MURDER

8. Wotan puts his Valkyrie daughter Brunhilde to sleep on a big rock and surrounds it with fire because she

disobeyed him (she tried to save Siegmund – don't ask). – PARENTAL ABUSE

9. Siegmund and Sieglinde's son, whose name is Siegfried, is raised alone in the woods by another repulsive dwarf named Mime, whose ulterior motive is to get Siegfried to fight Fafner, who is now a dragon, and get the Ring for him, Mime, after which he, Mime plans to poison Siegfried. – CHILD ABUSE, CONSPIRACY TO COMMIT ROBBERY AND MURDER

10. Siegfried, who is stupid, kills Fafner and gets the Ring and the magic helmet. He is too dumb to know what he has, so he's not likely to become Master of the Universe. Fafner's dragon blood gives him the ability to hear people's thoughts, and he eavesdrops on Mime's evil mind, then kills him. Siegfried goes to the big fire-surrounded rock and wakes up Brunhilde, who is the half-sister of his parents. They fall in love. – MURDER DURING THE COMMISSION OF A ROBBERY, MURDER OF STEPFATHER, INCEST AND BEING A STUPID JERK

11. There is more murder, deception and mayhem, after which the whole world is destroyed by fire, which is fed by Brunhilde throwing a torch over Siegfried's funeral pyre, then walking into it leading her horse. – ARSON, SUICIDE, ANIMAL CRUELTY

You can't make this stuff up, but Wagner did. To his credit, he got a lot of it from old Germanic mythology, but he expanded on it big time.

Wagner needed some serious therapy. Unfortunately, he died in 1883, just a little bit too early to take advantage of Siegmund Freud, who was just getting started.

CHAPTER 6: THE FRENCH AND THE RUSSIANS

Once everybody else saw that the Italians had come up with a Good Thing, other countries wanted to get in on it. I already covered the Germans in an earlier lesson, so I won't talk about them anymore. German composers weren't the only non-Italians who wrote operas although they probably thought they were the only ones worth bothering about.

The French got into the act pretty early, even though their most famous opera composer in those years was an Italian expatriate named Giovanni Battista Lulli. Because he knew the French hated foreigners, and he was making good money in France, he turned himself into Jean Baptiste Lully and pretended he didn't know any Italian songs when anyone asked him to play at a party.

Another famous French opera composer was a misplaced German Jew named Jacques Offenbach. He wrote a lot of French operettas and one opera, *The Tales of Hoffman.* In typical German fashion, the opera has spooky scenes and evil supernatural stuff, but it's in French and Offenbach was thoroughly French by then, so the Germans can't claim it as one of theirs even if they want to, which they probably don't, although with the Germans you never know.

The Germans have a way of sneaking into things, even when people try to ignore them.

The most famous of French operas is *Carmen,* by Georges Bizet. People think this opera is Spanish, because Bizet did a good job of imitating Spanish music in it and it takes place in and around Seville, which is in Spain, in case you don't know. For some reason, more than one French composer has written Spanish-style music. Italian composers dabbled in it once in a while, but they didn't make a habit of it.

Carmen is popular because the story is easy to follow and it's full of passion and sex and pathos and everything else that makes a ripping good story. Opera singers like it because it gives them plenty of chance to show off. For an opera singer, showing off in front of an audience is the main reason for existing. If you don't believe this, just try upstaging one of them sometime. You'll only get a chance to try that once. The resulting retaliation will hurt. A lot.

Carmen is a story about a one-sided love affair between a lively Spanish gypsy named Carmen and a Basque soldier in the Spanish army, whose name is Don Jose. It's one-sided because for her it's a fling and for him it's your-my-woman-and-you're-stuck-to-me-whether-you-want-to-be-or-not-because-if-I-can't-have-you-nobody-will obsession. To add to the confusion, the soldier has a virginal girlfriend from back home named Micaëla, who he was supposed to marry before he ran off with someone more fun.

The problem is that Carmen, the gypsy, gets the flaming hots for the toreador Escamillo, who is a lot more exciting than Don Jose. When Don Jose, a Mama's boy in addition to a psychopath, has to go home to see his dying mother, Carmen takes advantage of his absence to abscond and take up with Escamillo. Don Jose finds her and asks her to come back to him. She tells him, "No!" in several different ways and finally yells at him to take his damned ring back and get lost. Instead of getting lost, he stabs her to death. This is the end of the opera and the end of Carmen. We get the feeling Jose won't be around much longer, either.

All this is sung to some pretty exciting music, full of well-known tunes, some of which have been recycled and used elsewhere. "I didn't know that was from an opera!" is one reaction that people give when they hear Carmen's *Habanera* sung in its original form. But yes, it is from an opera. And the original words to Escamillo's *Toreador Song* are NOT "Toreador, don't spit on the floor …." It's important to know that.

I haven't forgotten about the Russians.

Russian composers got into the act of writing operas in the 19th Century and never really stopped, even though in the 20th Century the Communists were watching them to make sure they were not imitating degenerate composers from the West. Composers like Tchaikovsky, Rimsky-Korsakov, Mussorgsky and Borodin had a lot of other problems, but at least they didn't have to worry about that because Communism hadn't been imposed on anyone yet.

Russians are a lot like Italians in that they like a lot of drama and emotion onstage. Tchaikovsky, for example, put a lot of both into his operas. Just catch the final scene of

Eugene Onegin, if you don't believe me. Although she has a hard time doing it, the heroine sends the leading man packing, to the great delight of the audience, because he's a selfish, irresponsible bastard and she's way too good for him.

All of that is done to some very lush, dramatic music, which makes everything better.

Russian opera composers are like Italians in another way, too. They are not long-winded like Wagner. They prefer an emotional drama, with good timing. This makes Russian operas easier for the neophyte opera-goer to swallow.

CHAPTER 7: FEMALE OPERA SINGERS AND OTHER WILD ANIMALS

A lot of people think female opera singers look like this:

Some of us look more like this:

Most of us are somewhere in between:

We've all heard the saying, "The opera isn't over until the fat lady sings." This is true. Even if sopranos can't always have the last word, we make enough noise during the few hours preceding the end to make sure that we get plenty of attention -- preferably more attention than anyone else. We keep track and we remember.

The joke goes: How many sopranos does it take to change a lightbulb? Only one. She holds the bulb while the world revolves around her. That pretty much nails it.

Mezzo-sopranos might have fewer opportunities to be the leading lady, but other than that they are capable of acting like sopranos.

Case in point: A female opera singer on tour overseas was staying at a 5-star hotel. She had been promised a room with a view of the famous river right across the street. Unfortunately, the room she was given only had a view of the next hotel. The woman threw a fit worthy of a toddler on Speed. The hotel manager solved the problem by having one of his workers go into one of the rooms with a view of the river and break the toilet. When the guest in that room reported the non-working plumbing, he was moved to another room. The toilet was fixed, the female opera singer was moved into the room with a view and everyone was happy except, possibly, the guy who had to move, unless he liked the view of the Hilton's swimming pool better than looking at a river. Depending on who was using the Hilton's swimming pool and in what kind of physical shape they were, the guy who had to move could have gotten the better deal.

No, that story is not about me. I wasn't even there, so don't get ideas.

You can't blame us. Female opera singers in general are not meek and humble. We are the human equivalent of bulldozers. Our personalities are a combination of estrogen, chutzpah, horniness, a touch of batshit craziness and balls. We don't actually have balls, but we act like we do, especially when someone tries to upstage us, take a job we are after or muscle in on a job we already have. It takes a lot of those proverbial balls to get up onto a stage with other singers who are just as ambitious, attention-hungry and crazy as we are and sing the most difficult music in the world while following the beat of some crazy conductor and trying to act at the same time.

That's about as easy as standing on your head in the middle of a busy avenue while peeling a banana with your feet, doing a hula and dodging bicycle messengers. Okay, I'm exaggerating. But you get the point. Singing opera is hard, and, to add insult to injury, audience members can be unforgiving if they don't like what a singer is doing. If you have paid good money for a ticket, you want the performance to be memorable for good reasons, not because you didn't like the soprano.

Actually, most of us are perfectly nice people as long as you don't do something stupid to set us off. If you do, all bets are off. And the worst times to aggravate us are before, during and right after a performance. Most of us are nervous before a performance, and in no mood for anything even remotely annoying. During a performance, the adrenalin is shooting around inside of us, along with heightened everything. Afterward, if the performance was a good one and we had an appreciative audience, we are on a huge high. Bring us down off that high at your own peril.

A poor process server learned this the hard way when he approached Maria Callas as she was coming offstage in Chicago after a performance of *Madama Butterfly.* He didn't just hand her the summons he had come to serve. He shoved it into her costume. She didn't just go ballistic on him, she went nuclear! It was over the top, but then she never did anything halfway. She was an opera singer. And the guy had caught her right after a performance. And he did something rude and disrespectful. You see my point.

On the positive side, most of us are fun to hang around with. Our desire to entertain people extends to everyday life, too. So if you want a good time, make friends with an opera singer.

CHAPTER 8: THE MEN

Male opera singers are just as crazy as the females, and just as likely to flay you alive if you get them mad, especially at performance time. Add to this an enormous ego and massive doses of testosterone, and you have a complete picture.

Like the females, male opera singers come in all sizes and shapes, the most popular being "larger than life."

This is what most of us wish our male colleagues looked like:

This is what we usually get:

Opera is not for sissies. These guys have balls of steel. They are also the horniest bunch of Casanovas you will ever come across, especially on long tours or engagements, away from their families and friends for weeks or even months at a time. Their colleagues, male and female, are just as randy, just as lonely and just as free of constraints as they are, and there are occasional groupies, not to mention that stone cold fox (or guy) who waits tables at some local cafe. It's always interesting to see who pairs off with whom on long tours. Some don't even bother to pair off; they just take on anyone who looks promising.

Even the ugly ones don't have any problem finding sex partners. A good male singing voice is the world's most effective aphrodisiac. Forget oysters or champagne. Just sing a few bars of a favorite love song in full, round tones that caress the eardrums of the temporary beloved, and presto! Instant seduction.

In other words, if you are thinking of marrying or becoming a partner of a guy who has ambitions to sing opera, don't expect him to be around the house all the time. And don't keep the home fires burning while he gallivants all over the place. If you want him to keep it where it belongs, you'll have to go with him wherever he gets hired, watch him like an eagle with binoculars and threaten to seriously hurt anyone who tries to get his attention.

When it comes to full-blown ego, male opera singers are world champions. That thing in their throats that makes it possible for them to make loud, gorgeous tones also sends vibrations into their heads and rearranges their brain cells, giving delusions of grandeur. It sends the same vibrations downstairs, doubly awakening and charging their erotic parts and sending hormones squirting all through their bloodstreams.

Onstage, the male singer expects to be the main object of the audience's attention and love. This puts him in direct opposition to the female opera singer, who is after the same thing. The resulting love-hate relationship makes the lives of opera company administrators very interesting. If the man and the woman also have something hot and heavy going on offstage, things become really complicated, especially if one or the other or both of them are married to other people who, at the time, are off in some other place and unable to complain.

The great soprano Birgit Nilsson and the great tenor Franco Corelli did NOT have anything hot and heavy going offstage, but they did have an onstage rivalry. They were often cast together in Puccini's opera *Turandot*. At one point late in that opera, the tenor is supposed to kiss the soprano with great passion and she is supposed to melt in his arms. Mr. Corelli complained to the General Manager of the Metropolitan Opera about Ms. Nilsson, and was told that, instead of kissing her, he could bite her. Mr. Corelli apparently told Ms. Nilsson about this advice, because the next day she called the office and, with her delicious sense of humor, told the General Manager that she couldn't sing her next performance because she had rabies!

Going back several decades before that, Enrico Caruso and Geraldine Farrar were often paired together onstage at the Met. Most of the time it was amicable enough, but then there was the time that Miss Farrar had just come back from Hollywood, where she had made a silent movie version of *Carmen,* and found herself onstage singing the opera with Caruso. Inspired by her work on the movie, she gave him a very hard slap at one point. You aren't supposed to do that onstage. Onstage slaps have to be faked, so that nobody gets hurt or surprised. Caruso didn't like the unpleasant surprise, for which nobody can blame him, and a backstage argument ensued. Fortunately, management intervened, amicable relations were restored and the Met's biggest box office attraction was not split up. Everyone was happy.

Male opera singers have their moments, too, and you bother them at those times at your own peril. Caruso, who was normally friendly, good hearted and likeable, suffered from miserable stage fright. He could be a roaring bear backstage before a performance. It was a tribute to his usual loveable nature that he didn't lose any friends that way. A tenor of my acquaintance once had a visit from his agent backstage before a performance, to tell him that someone important was in the audience. My tenor friend, who was ready to give his best performance anyway, went ballistic. He didn't need that kind of mental distraction before going onstage, and he let his agent know it. This tenor guy, too, was one of the nicest people ever, as long as you weren't doing something that could sabotage one of his performances.

Sopranos, tenors, mezzo-sopranos, contraltos, baritones, and basses do manage to make beautiful music together onstage, which is why so many people become hooked on opera.

CHAPTER 9: SOPRANOS AND MEZZO-SOPRANOS

I used to have a wonderful vocal coach who, when she heard me say something that she thought was dumb (which was half the time), would yell, "Stupid f***-head soprano!"

Sopranos are expected to be ditzy. Supposedly, the vibrations that buzz through a soprano's head whenever she sings a high note result in the rearrangement of brain cells. My coach must have assumed that I, a big-voiced soprano, was brain-dead. Many people who know me say she was right.

Most people don't know or care, but there are different kinds of sopranos. These range from *coloratura* sopranos*[12]

[12] Also known as "tweety birds," by other singers, who wish they could sing like that.

with their light voices and stratospheric high notes to *dramatic* sopranos, who can't sing as high but make up for it with voices that can peel the paint off a wall two blocks away. The loudest of the *dramatic* sopranos are the *Wagnerian* sopranos. These are the spear-carrying ladies in the long dresses and Viking helmets, bellowing out war cries or setting everyone on fire. In between, there are *lyric* sopranos and *spinto* sopranos, including me, the author of this book. We *spintos* have a lot of fun because we are basically *lyric* sopranos with punch. We get to make the audience cry with heart-melting scenes and take the paint off a wall two blocks away at the same time. It doesn't get any better than that.

By the way, your Aunt Judy who sings solos with the church choir is a *lyric* soprano, but not in the same league. Opera singers have to be able to project to the last row of a theater, over an orchestra, without a microphone. Put a real operatic *lyric* soprano with Aunt Judy, and Aunt Judy will last about two notes before being swallowed up like a mouse in a cage with a hungry snake.[13]

Sopranos get to sing almost all of the leading female roles in opera. Our characters are love-struck, long-suffering, self-sacrificing, abused, dying, psychotic because

---

[13] Church sopranos and other non-operatic singers who choose to sing with an opera singer don't know the mess they are stepping into. It is the duty of every opera singer to try to out-sing everyone else who is singing at the same time, because it's *fun*. We expect other opera singers to react in kind, and they almost never disappoint us. If you don't believe me, go onto YouTube and find a video of one of the Three Tenors concerts, where all three of them are singing together. If that isn't competitive singing, nothing is!

of abusive relatives and all kinds of other things that get loads of sympathy from everyone in the audience.

This brings us to the subject of mezzo-sopranos. Mezzos have voices that are lower pitched than sopranos. The term *mezzo-soprano* means "half-soprano" in Italian. Why they are called that, I don't know. It's insulting, really. It must be an Italian thing. I wouldn't describe most mezzo voices as "half" by any means, especially when one of them is singing near me. Mezzos can break eardrums as well as any other opera singers.

They also come in categories, from *coloratura* to *dramatic*. Some of them get tired of being in the supporting cast and drift into soprano repertoire occasionally, which makes things interesting, if confusing.

Unlike sopranos, mezzos are expected to be more or less level-headed. In truth, they are just as ditzy and outlandish as sopranos, but I never heard anyone say, "Stupid, f***-headed mezzo" to anyone. It just isn't done. The stress of having to appear relatively normal for an opera singer is hard on the poor mezzo, especially when she sees sopranos and tenors getting away with murder. Occasionally, they break down and exhibit the same traits, but they soon learn to put a lid on it, so as not to buck tradition.

Mezzos usually end up playing villains, old women, witches or sluts. Sometimes they play men. This is a throwback to the *castrati* of the 17th Century. *Castrati* were the rock stars of their day, except they sang opera instead. They were men whose testicles had been removed when they were boys to preserve their high singing voices. For some reason, people back then thought the sound of a grown man singing soprano was really cool. Fortunately for the male sex and their privates, this fashion eventually faded, and parents stopped turning their sons into eunuchs in hope that they would become rich and famous. Female singers ended up taking up the slack. As a result, mezzos have to wear pants onstage a lot.

No, it isn't logical. End of discussion.

It might seem that mezzos get shafted, but, in a way, they get the better deal. They don't have as many roles to choose from, and they usually have to play second banana, but their roles are juicy and often much more interesting than those that sopranos end up with. It's the case of the villain or the character role vs. the moony, virtuous heroine. Take, for example, the opera *Aïda*, by Giuseppe Verdi:

<u>Soprano</u>

Name of Character: Aïda

Profession: Daughter of the King of Ethiopia (but nobody knows this). A slave in the court of the Pharaoh of Egypt, having been captured in war.

Nice. Sweet. Homesick. In love with Radames, the leader of the Egyptian army (which isn't easy, because he keeps going to war against her country). I mean STUPID in love. Self-sacrificing and patriotic. Also suicidal.

Mezzo-Soprano

Name of Character: Amneris

Profession: Daughter of the Pharaoh of Egypt. In line to be Queen.

Spoiled. Smart. Ambitious. Super smart. In love with Radames and will do anything to snare him. Devious. Gets what she wants or else. Goes into huge emotional meltdown when her actions come back to bite her in the ass in a big way.

You tell me. What part would you rather play?

CHAPTER 10: TENORS

Yes, tenors get their own chapter. You'll see why.

Tenors and sopranos are natural enemies, passionate lovers or both. Whatever the state of the relationship, it is never dull.

Tenors are the rock stars of opera. They sing almost all of the leading roles and they can sing higher than the other males, at least the ones that use their natural voices. Countertenors, most of whom are baritones who have figured out that they can make more money by singing Handel operas with an overdeveloped falsetto, can sing higher than tenors and even a few sopranos. To the mind of a tenor, though, this doesn't count because (1) singing in falsetto is cheating and (2) countertenors are weird.

To many people the phrase "the mind of a tenor" is an oxymoron. Tenors are supposed to be stupid. All opera singers have a reputation for being stupid, but tenors have a reputation for being the most moronic of the morons. In truth, none of us are stupid, including the tenors. We're eccentric. We are obsessive laryngeal hypochondriacs and we get hysterical over clogged sinuses. Add to this that we are the kind of people who like to show off in front of huge crowds, we are somewhat uninhibited, and our ideas of how something should be done don't always mesh with those of conductors, stage directors and administration. The term "idiot"* just naturally comes out of the mouths of people who have to deal with us.[14] For some reason, people think that tenors are more eccentric than the rest of us, probably because sopranos love to spread that bit of slander around. (See "natural enemies' and "love-hate," above.)

Opera singers in general and tenors in particular are often said to have resonance where their brains ought to be. It is easy to forget that that is scientifically impossible when you hear some tenors talk.

---

[14] Also "f***head, bitch and a**hole, without the asterisks

Almost all romantic leads in almost all classic operas are written for tenors. This is ironic, because tenors are not known for their good looks. With notable exceptions, the best tenor voices often belong to the short, dumpy guys. This can be comical when the soprano is taller than the tenor and the two of them are singing a love duet. Most of the tall, great looking male opera singers are either baritones or basses, and they are almost always relegated to playing villains (baritones) or old men (basses). Opera is not logical.

What makes things REALLY ironic, to the point of head scratching, is that a good tenor voice is a powerful female aphrodisiac. Even the short, fat guys can make women sigh and swoon when they come out with a couple of good high notes along with some silky tones leading up to them. I guess this is nature's way of giving tenors an even chance of getting laid backstage.

This even chance is useless, though, to tenors who hold to the belief that they have to abstain from sex for a few days before a performance, to make sure their voices are in working order. This must be torture, because, along with baritones and basses, tenors are among the most randy males who walk on two legs. No sacrifice is too great for a good onstage performance, although the man's wife, partner or girlfriend might not agree.

There are other tenors who believe that sex in the dressing room right before going onstage oils the voice very nicely. If the evening's soprano[15] is of the same mind, some interesting goings-on can result, especially if one or both of them is married or otherwise tied to another person.

---

[15] In some cases the evening's baritone

As much as they love it, I have now given the tenors enough attention.

CHAPTER 11: BARITONES AND BASSES

Baritones are the sex gods of the opera world.[16] A baritone voice and hot looks seem to go together. The irony is that baritones, the hottest guys on the opera stage, are usually relegated to the roles of villains. When they are not playing villains, they are somebody's father, brother, sidekick, best friend, hunchback clown, or whatever. The baritone never gets the heroine, even if he sees her first. He takes a lot of cold showers. The short, fat tenor gets her, even if someone has to die, usually the tenor or the woman, or both.

It isn't all that bad, though. Baritones get to play interesting characters and sing some of the best show-stopping music in the whole operatic repertoire and, even if they don't get lucky onstage, they see plenty of action offstage. Sometimes they even get to have some fun

[16] The slang term for a hot looking baritone is "barihunk." Remember that. It will be on the quiz, if I ever make one up.

throwing the soprano around onstage. This is more fun for the baritone than for the soprano, and it is wise for him not to get carried away. Female opera singers pack a punch, and they don't mind using it, even on baritones.

The audience's suspension of disbelief is stretched to the breaking point when a romantic hero is played by Short, Fat Tenor and a lecherous villain is played by Sexy Baritone. The soprano has to do all her romantic scenes with Short, Fat Tenor and give Sexy Baritone the equivalent of, "F*** off, you disgusting worm!" It is my theory that this is how sopranos got their reputation for being touched in the head, or at least nearsighted.

Once in a blue moon a baritone gets to play a sexy part. The best example is Mozart's *Don Giovanni*. Don Giovanni is a baritone, and his little black book has 1,003 names of his Spanish girlfriends alone. He also has a boatload more in Italy, Germany, France and Turkey. In the course of the opera, he fails with every woman he tries to make time with and ends up in Hell, but he's just having a bad couple of days. He has had a lot of fun traveling around Europe: the original sex tour.

Like baritones, a lot of basses are handsome and sexy looking. Others are short and fat, like tenors. The short and fat ones often specialize in comic roles. The tall, handsome, sexy ones usually end up playing someone's father, a priest, a king or an old man. Also like baritones, basses get some great music to sing and some interesting characters to play, which makes up for having to put on all that makeup and pretend you're not as good looking as you are.

Basses with high enough voices will often tackle the role of Don Giovanni, too. It's hard to resist playing a guy with 2,065 names in his black book.

Basses who specialize in comic roles not only get to be funny, they get to impress audiences with things like rapid patter singing, which I hope, for the singers' sakes, is easier than it sounds, although I suspect it isn't.

It's a sure applause winner.

CHAPTER 12 - NON-SINGING PERFORMERS

Supernumeraries

"Supers" are the extras of the opera world. For a pittance, they are willing to get into costume and makeup and: (1) stand or sit around, looking pretty; (2) stand or sit around looking scruffy; (3) stand or sit around looking innocuous; (4) carry stuff around; (5) march around; (6) carry rifles and shoot someone; (6) hold stuff; (7) run around, or (8) do whatever they are needed to do. They are often referred to as "spear carriers." The director, who often ends up acting like a traffic cop when dealing with supers, can only hope that they will remember, from one rehearsal to the next, what they are supposed to do and with what, and do it right.

Unless they are aspiring singers just looking for a little extra money and a chance to get close to some stars, chances are very good that supers don't have a clue as to what the opera is all about. Woe to the stage director who doesn't take this into account.

There is one story that may or may not have happened, but that has become legendary operatic lore. It seems that one of the big American opera companies was doing a production of Puccini's *Tosca*. I won't go into the story of this opera because it would take too long. Suffice it to say that, at the end of Act III, a firing squad comes onstage, takes its position and shoots the leading tenor, in the presence of the leading soprano, who has been fooled into thinking this is going to be a fake execution by the baritone, whom she murdered at the end of Act II. When it hits her that the tenor really is dead, and the baritone's elite cops come running up to grab her after finding the body that SHE killed, she goes berserk and kills herself by jumping off a parapet and splattering herself on the pavement below.

In this one production, the supers who were hired to play the firing squad were some local college boys who had no clue what *Tosca* was all about and weren't interested enough to find out on their own. During rehearsals, they kept asking the director what they were supposed to do. The director, who was concentrating on the principal singers, kept putting them off. To make matters more complicated, there was no dress rehearsal because various problems had come up during the rehearsal period. The firing squad were given some last-minute instructions, including "Exit with the principals." This was probably the most regrettable order the director ever gave.

Apparently, the firing squad guys hadn't been paying any attention to anything the principals had been doing in rehearsal, because when the time came they "shot" the leading soprano instead of the leading tenor and were surprised to see the tenor fall down. At that point, they should have exited the stage, but nobody had told them that. Instead, they remembered that they were supposed to exit with the principals. The problem was that the principals were not exiting. The tenor was lying on the floor, other people were entering, and the soprano ran to the parapet, stood there and sang her last line. The firing squad did the only thing they could think to do. When the leading soprano jumped off the parapet, they all jumped after her![17]

[17] Vickers, Hugh. *Great Operatic Disasters.* Copyright 1979 by Hugh Vickers. This is still in print, and easily available, and it is hilarious.

Small opera companies often have loyal, opera-loving amateurs who are thrilled to get into costume and take part in performances as amateur supernumeraries. I am thinking of the now-defunct Amato Opera Theater, which used to grace a corner of Manhattan's Bowery. This company operated for many decades in a tiny, 104-seat jewel of a theater, under the musical and stage direction of Anthony Amato. I had the privilege of working with them back when I was an operatic newbie, and it was one of the best experiences of my younger life. Tony Amato was a joy to work with, and he knew just about everything about how to perform in opera. If you couldn't learn from him, you couldn't learn anywhere.

Because the building was so small, the stage was tiny, with no space in the wings. Not to be defeated by mere lack of space, Tony Amato set his improvisational skills to high. The Triumphal Scene in *Aïda?* No problem! Just because it required a cast of thousands at the Metropolitan Opera didn't mean that the Amato Opera Theater couldn't have a parade, too. Tony just had all of his wonderful, volunteer supers enter from the back of the theater and march up the aisle. It was kind of impressive, in its own way. For the audience, it was opera up close and personal.

Animals

One particular group of supernumeraries deserves special mention: animals.

Many members of non-human species have found themselves on the stages of opera houses around the world. These include horses, donkeys, elephants, dogs, lions and whatever else tickles the fancy of the director and is likely to please the audience, especially if the production is a big, outdoor extravaganza.

One thing about animals is that a stage is not a natural habitat for any of them. It isn't a natural habitat for humans, either, but that's beside the point. Those of us who are so inclined can wrap our brains around the situation and enjoy being a center of attention. Animals can't do that. When they are suddenly thrust out in front of a big crowd of strange humans, under hot lights and with more strange humans standing around them, they can get very nervous.

When they get nervous, they often react, sometimes in very messy ways.

In other words, if you are going to parade horses and elephants across a stage, you had better have a cleanup crew ready in the wings with shovels and mops.

It is wise for stage directors to be aware, also, that the sight of an animal depositing a pile of manure is going to upstage anything else that is going on. This could result in some very unhappy principal singers, who are of the opinion that the audience's attention should be on *them*, not on a nervous elephant relieving herself.

That said, it is true that the sight of a live animal onstage can be very entertaining and even moving, in a way. Fake animals just don't make it onstage. One case in point is the Metropolitan Opera's recent staging of Wagner's *Der Ring des Nibelungen.* In the final scene of the final act of the final opera in this series, the leading soprano, Brunnhilde, walks or rides into the funeral pyre of her one true love, Siegfried, bringing her horse with her. Of course, the fire is not real, so no animals or humans are harmed in the staging of this opera – at least not on purpose.

For some reason, the Metropolitan Opera used a robotic horse for this. Sitting in the audience watching this, I wanted to regress to childhood and yell, "Fake! Fake!" You don't do that at the Met, though, no matter how immature you are feeling at the moment.

The wonderful Australian soprano Marjorie Lawrence had a real horse to work with when she sang the role of Brunnhilde at the Metropolitan Opera. She had grown up with horses, and was a skilled rider. Against the wishes of her director, who had forbidden it, she didn't just lead the horse into the "flames." She mounted the horse and *rode* into them! She had a lot of moxie, and it worked. People loved it.

One of the funniest animal appearances that I remember seeing was during a performance of Rossini's *The Barber of Seville* at the Metropolitan Opera, many years ago. The great bass Fernando Corena was singing the role of the villain, Dr. Bartolo. In Act I, he made his entrance wearing one of those fancy old-fashioned white wigs and walking a poodle on a leash. The poodle and the wig had the same haircut.

You had to be there.

Of course, nobody asks the animals if they want to appear on an opera stage. Nobody even asks them if they like opera. For example, my cat gives me a look best reserved for a visiting zombie, then leaves the room if I start to sing. I don't think she'd appreciate being stuck in the middle of *Carmen* or *The Barber of Seville*. It's something to think about.

Dancers

Opera and ballet have been joined at the hip for centuries. Every decent-sized opera company has a ballet along with a chorus and an orchestra. Even some of the tiny companies that are trying to operate on a budget the size of a miser's tip will try to bring in a dancer or two on occasion.

Some operas have a lot of dancing; some have none. Some operas have one big ballet scene in an otherwise dance-less piece. In classic French operas, a ballet scene is almost required. It just wasn't *French* if it didn't have a big ballet sequence somewhere, preferably not right at the beginning. Richard Wagner found this out the hard way, when he was invited to present his opera *Tannhäuser* in

Paris. He had already premiered this opera in Germany without a ballet, but to be a hit in Paris, he knew he had to put one in. Unfortunately, he put it smack at the beginning of Act I, instead of in Act II, where people expected it to be put. The rich, upper-class boyfriends of some of the ballerinas had a habit of coming in late (because they *could*), and they were mad as hell that they had to be on time for this opera or they'd miss seeing their girlfriends onstage. The boyfriends made such a ruckus that Wagner got mad right back, took his opera and went home to Germany.

By the way, when *Tannhäuser* is performed nowadays, the ballet is still there, in Act I, and nobody complains.

Well, that depends. That particular ballet takes place in the home of the goddess Venus, and it's pretty sexy. Just how sexy depends on the costume designer and the choreographer. People who don't like operatic erotica might complain if too much skin is showing and/or the movements are too sensual. Of course, that depends on what people think is erotic. Oh, forget it! This is getting too complicated. You get the picture, I'm sure.

One famous ballet comes at the end of Act III of Ponchielli's opera *La Gioconda*. This is the "Dance of the Hours." If you have ever seen Walt Disney's *Fantasia*, you will remember a troop of hippopotamuses in tutus, alligators and a few other species tripping their way through this ballet. You are a strong person if you can keep from laughing while watching human dancers performing this onstage. Walt Disney ruined this piece for generations to come.

On the other hand, how many of us get a chance to laugh at a ballet, especially one that is not meant to be funny and that is placed within a tragic opera? Such a chance should never be passed up.

Any singers who are onstage during a ballet have one job and one job only: stay out of the dancers' way, or take a chance on getting knocked on one's ass. Dancers need a lot of room, and if you don't give it to them you are taking your life into your hands, or at least risking a very embarrassing collision. Dancers may be skinny, but they're strong. You don't want to be hit by one, or kicked by one of those muscular legs. It will hurt.

Occasionally, chorus members will be asked to dance a little, but it will never be anything complicated. If you can find any choristers who can do anything more advanced than a two-step, you are a very fortunate director, indeed. Choristers don't like to have to dance, either, which complicates matters further. Sometimes it's better just to leave it alone and let the chorus sit the dance out.

CHAPTER 13: CONDUCTORS

Conductor, noun (kən dək tər): A musician who plays no instrument, yet always gets top billing.

Train Wreck, noun (trān rek): In ensemble music, the condition that results when one of the players or singers makes a wrong entrance, causing others to (a) follow suit in a disastrous domino effect or (b) stop singing or playing. The end result is a conductor about to go nuclear.>

An opera conductor is easy to spot. He's the guy standing on the podium in the orchestra pit, with his back to the audience, waving a stick at the orchestra and the singers and occasionally flashing a dirty look at someone or other. He is under the impression that he is the boss.

I use the pronoun "he" because 99.9 percent of working conductors in the world are men. This is one of the last bastions of male dominance. There are female conductors, but you rarely see one in an opera house or in front of a symphony orchestra. I have a theory that this is because most women don't want to stand with their backs facing a whole theater full of people, especially if they have fat butts. I could be wrong about this, and I probably am. It could also be that nobody wants to hire female conductors because everyone thinks it's a man's job, like running a forklift or taking out the garbage.[18]

Okay, so conductors like to think they are the boss. Technically, this is at least true in part, because it is his job to see to it that the orchestra musicians, the principal soloists and/or the choristers are performing the same measures of music at the same time and sounding good as they do it. This sounds like a big responsibility, and it is. Don't let that

---

[18] Both of these jobs can be handled by women, by the way. We just prefer to make men do anything involving lifting or filthy stuff.

fool you, though. Conductors love it. It's the ultimate ego trip.

The catch is that this can cause a certain amount of friction between the conductor and other people who also think they are the boss, such as stage directors and leading singers. Conductors get really nervous when they think the singers aren't looking at them. Singers hate to stare at the conductor, including veteran singers who know what they are doing by now. There is also such a thing as peripheral vision, which comes in handy when you want to see what the conductor is doing without staring at him like a cat stalking a laser beam. This makes singers look stupid, and nobody wants to look stupid in front of a bunch of people who have paid for tickets and don't want to see people looking stupid onstage. In addition, conductors have a bad habit of giving musical suggestions during staging rehearsals, when the stage director is busy filling the singers' brains with complicated movements and/or motivations. This is like someone attempting to slice your brain in half by reminding you, at the same time that you are trying to work out a complicated movement, that there is an eighth-note rest in the second measure at the top of page 95 after the word *morire*. The resulting brain cell clash always destroys a few of them. This is not good, because singers need all the brain cells they can get.

Like singers, opera conductors come in types:

1. The Dream. The Dream conducts the music with just the right *tempi* and knows where singers have to breathe, when to slow down, when to speed up, etc. He makes the orchestra sound great, and always with perfect balance. He gives the singers just enough freedom to give their best interpretations. Singers are lining up and begging to work with him.

2. The Racer. The Racer thinks that the faster the music is played the better. He isn't happy unless every singer onstage hyperventilates at some point during the performance. It's almost impossible for the onstage performers to do anything resembling an interpretation, because they are busy just trying to keep up with him. Singers will work with him if they need the money, but they don't like it.

3. The Old Guy. Everyone is lucky if he stays awake through a whole performance.

4. The Metronome. This guy's main characteristics are an inflexible beat and no nuances. Can we say boring? To the singers, he's just an idiot with a stick in his hands, a necessary aggravation on the way to the paycheck.

5. The Waver. The Waver's beat is so imprecise that it's anybody's guess what he's trying to get people to do. The orchestra is probably used to him by now and has figured out what all those waves and circles mean. The singers aren't so lucky. He is a train wreck waiting to happen.

If any of you conductors are reading this and are now pissed off, I have just one request. Please don't hurt me.

CHAPTER 14: STAGE DIRECTORS

The average opera has several principal singers, a few *comprimario* singers (opera speak for bit players), a chorus and sometimes dancers. Some supernumeraries might also be hired to carry big stuff, sit or walk around and look like they are part of the scenery, which they are.

Someone has to tell everyone where to go, so the company hires a stage director.

Back in the Golden Age, when singers ruled and all was right with the Universe, the main jobs of the stage director were to make nice stage pictures, make sure people didn't bump into each other and keep the singers happy so they would just sing already and stop complaining so much. If a singer didn't want to do something, he didn't have to do it. This is as it should be

By now, 2014, the crown has been passed from singers to conductors to stage directors. Singers who want to work have no choice but to follow directions and shut up, even when the director is being stupid. The problem is that most directors form their concepts without considering *who* is going to be onstage and what kind of shape the person is in. No matter how hard they try, singers can only do so much when it comes to fitting themselves into someone else's fantasy, especially if the singer's physical type isn't something the director wants to think about, let alone look at. Despite popular thought among musicians, singers have brains[19] and they can think, which means they form their

[19] Our brains are abnormal, but functional. We just have to give them rest so they won't overheat

own concepts. The chances of a singer's secret concept gelling with that being imposed by a stage director are about 1 in a zillion. As I said before, though, singers go along because they have to if they would rather spend their lives onstage rather than waiting tables.

There are singers who go along with a director during rehearsals, then do what they want in the performance. They are known as The Future Unemployed.

In other words, singers and stage directors are natural enemies. I'm a singer and I'm telling this, so I get to tell it my way. If you disagree with me, write your own damned book.

Like singers and conductors, stage directors come in different types. Most stage directors are men, although women are taking up this job in increasingly larger numbers. You don't have to stand with your rear end facing the audience to direct an opera. You do have to enjoy telling people what to do. Motherhood is a good training ground for this, although it is optional.

The different types of stage director are:

1. <u>The Traffic Cop</u>. This kind of director revels in moving large bunches of people around on a stage and creating epic spectacles. If he can toss in a horse or two just to show off, he will. Elephants are even better. As long as he gets the right people in the right spots at the right times, he doesn't care about such things as characterization or realistic acting. He leaves that up to the singers and doesn't even notice if their acting is good or bad as long as they end up in the right places onstage. His direction is often described as "park and bark."

2. The Choreographer. Unlike The Traffic Cop, the Choreographer is so concerned with detail that he plans out every tiniest movement and gesture that a singer makes, even to the point of what beat or chord on which the singer should move or gesture. The Choreographer will waste hours of rehearsal time driving everyone to insanity trying to get Uncoordinated Soprano to drop her fan on that one F-Major chord, after stepping precisely to the beat for one measure. If patiently going over and over that same action doesn't work, The Choreographer resorts to yelling and name-calling, reducing Uncoordinated Soprano to tears and making sure that she is terrified into paralysis whenever she sees him.

Which brings us to …

3. The Bully. This guy thinks that the best way to get people to do things the right way is to yell at them. Of course, it takes a lot of energy to holler at everybody, so some Bullies will choose one or two members of the cast to pick on, usually the one(s) who look like they can't fight back. The Bully will never pick on the soprano whose wealthy CEO uncle is bankrolling the production or the baritone who is the General Director's love interest of the month.

4. The Method Guy. This one will inspire the cast with all kinds of insights into the characters they are playing and create all kinds of backstories and motivations. He'll forget, though, to stage the performance so that the *audience* understands everything. The cast will have a great time, but the audience will leave the theater wondering what the hell they just saw, and why.

Speaking of what and why:

5. The Avant-Garde Enthusiast. This guy never heard the expression, "If it isn't broken, don't fix it." Any opera is fair game, no matter how classic and revered. This is the guy who will set Verdi's *Aïda* on a spaceship instead of in ancient Egypt, where it belongs. He won't pay any attention to the libretto (i.e. the words) of the opera, which he probably doesn't understand, anyway. Unfortunately, these guys are working all over the place, because everyone who has power in the opera world thinks this is the wave of the future. Except in very rare cases, it's a wave of stupidity.

Last but not least:

6. Every Singer's Ideal. This person is to be treasured as a precious pearl. He knows how to set up a good stage picture, and he does so. He also respects the singers, listens to them and, if they have any good ideas, lets them at least try them out in rehearsal to

> see if they work or not. He never yells at anyone. Even if his staging has a touch of the avant-garde, it makes sense, because he has thoroughly studied the libretto. He is as rare as a Buddha statue in a Catholic church.

The real miracle is that some kind of performance usually comes off. This depends on the professionalism and experience of the principal singers, the conductor, the chorus and the orchestra, especially when they are dealing with idiotic staging and impossible scenery. In a case like that, they just try to pull it off and hope the audience won't know how silly they are all feeling and how many jokes they are making about the director when he isn't around to say anything.

CHAPTER 15: THE SO-CALLED LIFE OF AN OPERA SINGER

Life upon the wicked stage ain't nothin' for a girl.

Ellie in Jerome Kern's and Oscar Hammerstein II's musical *Show Boat*[20]

People outside "The Business" are fascinated when they hear that someone is an opera singer. Either that, or they find it hilarious. It's an alien existence to most people. Sometimes it's an alien existence to us, too, but that's a whole other story.

For those of you who are really curious about what life on the operatic stage is like, here are a few glimpses. If you are not all that curious, please read this anyway. I like having readers.

You can't be an opera singer if you can't sing like one. Only being able to sing is not enough. Opera requires standing onstage in a theater and singing without a microphone, over a full-sized orchestra, without resorting to bellowing. You need *at least* a two-octave range, in a recognizable voice type, and the stamina to keep all this up through a two- or three-hour performance (not counting intermissions). In other words, you have to have a big, loud, wide-ranged, beautiful voice with a nice vibrato to begin with, after which you have to study for years to get it into shape. If you're smart, you'll keep on taking an occasional

[20] Notice how I gave all that proper credit.

voice lesson even after you are singing on the stage, just to keep in training. Why not? Athletes do it.

Oh, but there's more!

You have to be able to act, too. Well, let me qualify that statement. You have to at least be able to move around a stage without looking like a clumsy robot. The acting ability of opera singers ranges from genius to embarrassing, but the audience likes to see that you are, at least, trying to play a character up there, at the same time that you are singing the world's most difficult vocal music, trying not to forget any of your words, and trying not to trip over your costume or stab yourself with your sword.

Don't plan on having a normal life. Little things like marriage, family life, a permanent home somewhere that you actually get to be in a lot of the time and being able to spend holidays with your family become a lot harder to achieve the more you achieve your career. (Okay, scratch the family holiday. That can be a blessing, if you have relatives from Hell.) Working opera singers can end up either moving from place to place or getting hired in New York, Berlin and London[21] in the same month.

Don't get me started on auditions. I'll just say that they are a something like being in front of a firing squad without a blindfold or a cigarette.

---

[21] Or Minneapolis, Detroit and Fort Worth, if you're not quite in the New York, Berlin and London category

CHAPTER 16: AUDITIONS

Job applicants have interviews. Opera singers have auditions. Auditions are different than interviews, because they are sung, nobody has to ask any questions and nobody cares where you think you will be in five years.

That said, auditions are more complicated than they sound.

Before a singer even gets to the point of thinking about auditioning, certain preparations have to be done.

Audition Arias

By tradition, every American opera singer who wants to break into the business has to have a list of five arias that he or she can pull out and sing at any time, awake or half-asleep, sick or well (except for laryngitis, of course) and sound good. Again by tradition, this list has to contain at least one aria in Italian, one in German, one in French, and one in English. The remaining aria can be in any language, but Italian is the biggie, followed by German, then French, then English.

Opera singers are not expected to be able to speak all of those languages, but they are expected to be able to sing in them, with perfect pronunciation. At least, *American* opera singers are expected to sing in Italian, German and French with perfect pronunciation. European opera singers can come up with some strange sounds in languages that are not their native tongues, and nobody seems to care. On this side of the Atlantic, it's a case of American pride in believing we are able to do something better than anyone else in the world. On the other side, it's a case of sticking it to those upstart Yanks.

Having this kind of rock solid list is great, until somebody from some opera company decides to require something altogether different. In that case, the singer had better hope that he or she at least knows the piece and can give something resembling a performance of it. If not, there is the option of either cramming to learn the piece fast (if there is time) or faking it (if there is not.) Some singers have tried this. They have often begun to regret that choice after a couple of notes, and will continue to regret it for the rest of their lives, every time they remember it or someone brings it up.

Singers who are veterans with a long list of roles performed have the opposite problem: choosing just the right audition piece out of a long list of possibilities. On the other hand, a long resume makes a singer look good, or at least better than a beginner. This brings us to another problem. You can't get real experience unless someone hires you, but nobody wants to hire you if you have no real experience. In an effort to get around this, "emerging" singers will often pad their resumes to make it look like they have done more than they actually have done. This is a courageous (and desperate) thing to do, because it's very easy nowadays to check these things in about two minutes, and the people behind the audition table get a little peeved when they know someone is trying to deceive them. They have long memories, too. If they don't have long memories, they have files. Same thing.

Auditioning in Europe carries its own set of language problems, and it can get complicated. Take Germany and Austria, for example. In small and mid-sized houses, they usually perform everything in German, including Italian, French and Russian operas. They even do American operas in German. Imagine a bunch of Germans in blackface, performing *Porgy und Bess*. You get the idea. They also do American musicals in German. To most German directors in small houses, America is an exotic place filled with stereotypes and misinformation. This can result in some unintentionally funny or groan-worthy things, such as having Julie in Show Boat in complete blackface, instead of having her passing for white, as the script plainly indicates.[22]

On the other hand, the larger houses, especially the international houses, do their operas in the original language as a rule.

---

[22] Germans don't know what to make of African-Americans. This was brought home to me once when I was walking down the street of a German city with an African-American friend. People were staring at us. I commented on this, and my friend calmly explained to me that they were staring at *her*, and that she experienced that all the time. I guess you can't blame people for staring when they grew up in a place where they only saw other white people, but I thought it was rude and I felt bad for my friend that she had to put up with that.

In other words, an American singer auditioning in Giessen will sing in German no matter what, but if his agent sends him to Berlin he'd better sing that same Verdi aria in Italian, and it had better be good.

Confusing? Of course. Imagine what it's like if you're the *singer*.

Contrary to popular belief, singers are not stupid. It's just that we have our brains crammed with all kinds of crazy stuff in an effort to try to please everybody. This makes simple things like thinking much harder because all that other garbage takes up so much memory space. That's my opinion, and I'm sticking to it.

Audition Aria Advice

A singer's voice teacher, who hears him in a small studio, where, with great effort, s/he gets him to do heroic things with his voice because he's working hard on his technique, will often think that he can do those same heroic things with his voice when faced with an audience of people who are judging him.

Wrong!

In other words, voice teachers make lousy audition advisers.

There will always be coaches, pianists and master class teachers who will give the singer conflicting advice about just what kind of voice he has. ("You're definitely a spinto tenor." "Oh, but you're a lyric tenor and you shouldn't sing anything too dramatic.") This leaves the poor singer even more confused and insecure than he was to begin with, which was already pretty confused and insecure.

Once in a while a singer's voice will be so obviously in a certain category that everybody agrees on what he is. Even then, they won't agree on exactly what arias he should sing.

The problem is that we singers can't hear ourselves the way everyone else hears us. We hear our voices from the inside, and the sound we hear is entirely different than the sound that is coming out. We have to rely on other people to tell us how we sound, what sounds good when we sing it and what makes people wince in pain.

So we endure many years of conflicting advice, until we finally figure out ourselves what works and what doesn't, usually from the reactions we get from audition panels and, if we're lucky, opera audiences.

Audition Clothes

Male singers have an easy time with this, because they can show up to an audition wearing anything that looks good, be it a black turtleneck with black pants, a nice looking sport jacket over a white shirt and dress pants, or a suit. The rule here seems to be, "If you look better than you do at any other time and your shoes are polished, you're good to go."

The men don't have to wear makeup, either. They just have to make sure that if they have anything on their faces it looks like they trim it occasionally.

For women singers, the story is entirely different. What makes it even more interesting is that we get conflicting advice all the time. If you ask ten different experts about what to wear at auditions, you will get ten different opinions.

Certain things are understood. The dress should not be too long or too short. It should be somewhere in between casual and formal (think corporate attire or cocktail dress). It should be conservative, and not attention-grabbing, because you want the people hearing you to pay attention to YOU, not to your dress.

After that, all bets are off.

Here is an example. Let's say that Singer A has a great voice and she can knock people over with any of her 5 audition arias. She has to choose a dress to wear to an audition where she might have a shot at being hired if it goes well. The problem is that Singer A is slightly overweight, with a large behind and a slightly fat stomach. She can never find a dress that fits well both on the top and on the bottom. She has tried everything. She has three dresses in her closet that she has marked as audition dresses. One of them looks good everywhere else, but hugs her stomach. Another one is too loose on the top, and she has to pin it closed. Another one curves over her fat behind, but looks good in front. She has to decide which dress to wear, and what she can use to accessorize it that will minimize whatever glaring figure flaw the dress is pointing out to the world.

She sends pictures of herself to her voice teacher, a friend who is the director of one of those tiny workshop companies and the photographer who took her publicity photo. She gets three different opinions, the most useless one from the photographer, who prefers the dress that is loose on the top because it shows cleavage and he's a breast man.

As with the choice of arias, the female opera singer often finds out from trial and error what dress works for auditions.

The Audition Itself

Auditions tend to have the same format:

1. The singer shows up and lets people know s/he is there.
2. There is a nervous wait, while singers who came earlier go first.
3. The singer is called into the audition space, and someone asks what s/he will sing OR chooses something from the singer's list.
4. The singer gives his/her music to the accompanist and sings.
5. Sometimes s/he is asked to sing again. More often than not, s/he only hears "Thank you," and is expected to leave.
6. The singer leaves the audition space.

Individual members of audition panels have different ways of reacting to singers, including:

1. Staring into space and looking bored;
2. Staring down at the table and looking bored;
3. Staring into space and conducting with one hand;
4. Looking through some singer's resume (hopefully the resume of the one who is singing);
5. Yawning and trying to stay awake;
6. Whispering to each other;
7. Whispering to each other and passing paper back and forth;
8. Letting the singer finish his/her aria, then making him/her stand at the piano feeling like a fool for what feels like an eon before finally looking up and saying, "Thank you."

Occasionally, one of them will surprise the singer and look interested. Even less occasionally, the singer will be treated to compliments, questions about his/her career, and other signs of interest. This doesn't always mean that the singer gets the job, but at least the singer leaves the audition feeling good. Once in a while, the singer will get the job. Once in a lifetime, the singer might not be hired right away, but will be at a later date. Getting hired is what makes the whole insane process worthwhile.

If the audition panel didn't fall all over the singer at the audition, chances are good that, a few weeks later, the dreaded PFO letter will arrive. This is usually a polite but impersonal letter giving some generic reason why the singer was rejected. Nobody ever tells the singer exactly why s/he didn't make it ("You're too tall for our tenor." "You remind me of my ex-husband." "I fought with your voice teacher." "We just didn't like you."). Most of the time, the singer never finds out.

Once in a while, something funny happens at auditions. I was in the middle of singing a beautiful Verdi aria on the stage of the Liederkranz Club Concert Hall in New York City. The man who was hearing auditions had rented it for the purpose. My agent was also present. In the middle of the aria, a workman walked into the hall, saw what was going on and stopped. He waited there for a moment, hoping I would finish, but it was not a short aria. The workman interrupted me politely and proceeded to ask us how to get to another part of the building. Apparently, he usually used the concert hall stage as a shortcut. He was advised by the wonderful British gentleman who was hearing me that we couldn't answer his question, so the workman apologized again for disturbing us and left, having decided to ask help from someone in the office.

My agent laughed and shook his head, and the gentleman hearing the auditions made a polite comment. I started my aria again, but whatever atmosphere I had managed to set up had been irrevocably broken. After I sang, the gentleman asked me some questions and showed some interest, but no, I didn't get the job.

Frequently Asked Questions

Here is a list of frequently asked questions, along with answers you might get from a singer who is in the mood to be snarky.

Can you break glass with your voice? No. Nobody can do that. If you ever find anyone who can, please warn me ahead of time, because I won't want to be standing in front of him when he opens up with one of those pinging notes. If he can break glass, think of what he can do with my fragile brain cells.

How many hours a day do you practice? I practice until my neighbors start throwing rocks through my window. (In other words, I don't get as much opportunity to practice as I would like, and I'm not about to let you know that.)

Where do you sing? I'm like a streetwalker. I perform for whoever pays me. I travel around a lot. So you won't have to worry that I'll commandeer you into coming to my next performance. It's in Tokyo.

What do you think of Luciano Pavarotti? I don't know. I never met the man and, considering that he's dead, I don't think I'll get an opportunity now. I do love his singing, and I'm sorry that he was silenced so soon.

Is it true that opera singers are temperamental? No. And if you ask that again I am going to kick you in the ass.

What advice can you give to someone who wants to have a career as an opera singer? Find something else to do that has less aggravation and pays better.

I hope that you have all enjoyed this little book about opera, and have gotten some good laughs out of it, as well as (maybe) learned a little. If it tweaks your curiosity enough to make you want to check out your local opera company, or just makes you stop and watch a little when they show an opera on PBS, my work has not been in vain.

If not, I hope you just got some laughs.

ENCORE 1: THE BIG AUDITION

Flash Fiction

Oh wow! Oh shit! I'm actually going to get up onto that stage and sing for the heads of the Metropolitan Opera. Me! What am I doing here? I don't belong here. What am I thinking? Of course, I belong here. People who know what they are talking about have been telling me for years that I should be singing at the Met and I believe it. Really, I do.

Okay. Concentrate. Better go over the words of what I'm going to sing. *Vissi d'arte, vissi d'amore. Non feci mai male ad anima viva.* What comes next? Fuck! I can't blank out like this! Oh yes: *Con man furtiva, quante miserie connobbi aiutai.* I've sung this a gazillion times and never forgotten the words. I won't forget them today.

Wow! That soprano who's up there now sounds pretty good. I'm glad she's a coloratura and not a *spinto*. She won't be competition.

Damn! Why is it so cold in here? Why didn't I bring my scarf? I'm going to sing on the stage of the Met, and I'm breathing cold air into my throat. I'd better check my voice out. HummmMMMmmm. Okay. It's still there. I'll just put my hand over my face to keep out the cold air. Why are those stagehands laughing at me? Haven't they ever seen a singer before?

Oh, come on! Why am I so friggin' nervous? I've been preparing for this for fifteen years. I've sung leading roles all over the place. I know all my music inside out. This is just another theater. No big deal.

Yes, it is a big deal! This is the MET, for Pete's sake! You sing here, you've made it. Fail this audition and I might not get another chance, ever. It seats 4,000 people. A stage as big as a city block. Shit, my hand is shaking. If my hand is shaking, my voice will probably shake. One shaky hand and my whole career is over.

I'm making myself nervous again! Stop it! You're going to do fine! Take some nice slow deep breaths and relax. One … two … three … ohmmmmm. Good. Much better.

Ooh, there's a mirror over there. Let's see. Makeup looks great. Hair looks fine. Dress fits just right. Boy, am I fat! I have a rear end like a beach ball. What if they turn me down because I'm too fat? Everybody keeps telling me how nobody wants to hire overweight opera singers anymore. What if the Met already has its quota of fat sopranos? I hate my shoes. What if they hate my shoes, too? What if I walk out there and stumble or say something really stupid like I did that time in Heidelberg?

Okay. Calm down. They HIRED me in Heidelberg, remember?

Con man furtiva … I have it in my brain now.

They're calling my name. Here goes. Stand tall, walk with confidence and act like you think you're the greatest soprano in the universe.

Yes, here I am!

ENCORE 2: TENORS AND BULLETS

This is a true story. I am not making it up. I was there, and I saw the whole thing.

The opera was Puccini's *Tosca,* produced by The Israel National Opera in their home theater, which had once been the Israeli Parliament (the "Knesset") building. The opera house was sandwiched between the beach and Tel Aviv's Red Light District. From 1978 – 1982, I was one of the company's leading sopranos. During that time, I broadened my repertoire, got great reviews in both local and international publications and made friends with a lot of people, including some of our immediate neighbors in the Red Light District. Most of them were male transvestites. (They were better dressed than I was and they probably made more money.) I was nice to them, which was wise. They got rough with anyone who disrespected them, from customers to bratty teenagers. I respected them, and they liked me.

All of that has nothing to do with the story I am going to tell. I just thought you'd find it interesting.

Okay. So the performance of Puccini's *Tosca* went without a hitch almost to the end. I was not in this performance. I shared the leading role with another soprano, a Romanian woman. She was singing that night, and I was watching from behind the last row of the orchestra section of the house.

Somebody dies in most operas, but in Puccini's *Tosca* all three of the leading characters bite the dust. The tenor gets his comeuppance via firing squad, just before the end of the opera. This requires precise timing and sound effects. In our case, the sound effects were provided by a little old guy named Milo, who stood backstage with a pistol loaded with blank bullets. He would shoot it at the right time, the tenor would fall down, the "firing squad" (a few chorus guys, equipped with old, plugged-up rifles) would leave the stage and the opera would continue to its end. Simple, right?

On this fateful night, Milo's gun failed to go off.

Maestro Tarski, the conductor, held the orchestra on a drum roll, waiting for the shot.

Milo kept trying to shoot the gun, which still failed to go off.

Maestro Tarski held the drum roll some more.

Milo, who was determined to shoot that damned gun, kept trying.

Maestro Tarski and the tenor could not see Milo, and Milo could not see them. Nobody knew what anyone else was doing.

Maestro Tarski finally shrugged his shoulders, figuring there would be no gun that evening, and gave a signal to the tenor. The tenor gave his usual realistic depiction of a man being shot to death. The "firing squad" began to file offstage.

Milo's gun went off.

The audience, which, up until then, had been absorbed in the tragic story, fell apart laughing.

It can only happen in opera.

OPERA TRIVIA

Caruso

The great Italian tenor Enrico Caruso did not die onstage, as many people think. He died at the age of 48, on a trip back to Italy, of an infection caused by a local doctor examining him with an instrument that was not sterilized. He had recently undergone surgery for an abscessed lung. There were no antibiotics in his day, or the original abscess could have been healed and he might have lived, and sung, for many more years. He died in 1921.

Caruso was a very talented caricaturist, who drew many caricatures of friends and even of himself. His friends were flattered. Some of his work can be seen in various books that have been written about him.

Caruso made many recordings, not only of operatic arias, duets and ensembles but of Neapolitan songs. He had been born in Naples and, as a youngster, had been a street singer, so those songs were second nature to him. He also recorded George M. Cohan's *Over There,* in an almost comically thick Italian accent.

Caruso never broke glass with his voice. Neither has anyone else. You can't do that with the human voice alone, even one that can sing in a big opera house, above a full orchestra, without microphones, and still be heard in the last row.

Common Questions Opera Singers Are Always Hearing

One of the most common questions addressed to opera singers is, "Can you break glass with your voice?" The answer is no, because, in spite of our sometimes inflated egos, we ARE only human.

Another common question is, "How many hours a day do you practice?" This always puts the singer on the spot, especially if it is asked in the presence of other singers, because it's very personal. Singers often find practicing difficult because of neighbors who complain about the noise, so practice time can vary from day to day. In addition, it's hard to make a living as an opera singer, and most of us have to work other jobs. This cuts into potential practice time. We prefer not to spread it around if we often can't practice as much as we should. For this reason, we usually answer this question by skirting around it.

Operatic Flops

Rossini's *The Barber of Seville* was a fiasco at its first performance, but not through any fault of Rossini or the opera. An older composer, Giovanni Paisiello, had already composed a highly successful *Barber of Seville*, and he was not about to let some upstart whippersnapper steal his glory. He had some of his fans attend the first performance of the new opera, make a lot of noise and disrupt it. That didn't do any good, though. Once the audiences actually got to see and hear Rossini's opera without rude interruptions, it became a bit hit. Rossini's opera is still very popular, while Paisiello's is only performed once in a great while, as kind of an academic curiosity.

Speaking of fiascos, Puccini's *Madama Butterfly* was also booed at its premiere. Puccini withdrew the opera, cut out some extraneous parts, and presented the new, compact version in another city. This time it was a hit, and it has remained one of the most familiar operas in the repertoire.

Composers and Librettists

Verdi and Puccini, both of whom had a spot-on sense of theatrical timing and what would work onstage, often drove their librettists crazy with demands to change this, add that, write this a certain way, etc. It worked, though, because both of these composers were musical and theatrical geniuses.

Wagner

Richard Wagner wrote his beautiful orchestral piece *Siegfried Idyll* as a birthday present for his wife, Cosima. Cosima was a daughter of another famous composer, Franz Liszt.

Verdi

As a young man, Verdi lost his wife and two children, all of whom died of illness. He went through a period of deep depression, which was only relieved when he was given the libretto of an opera called *Nabucco,* and persuaded to compose the music. He began by composing the beautiful, moving chorus *Va, pensiero*. The piece speaks of an exiled people longing for their beautiful homeland.

Verdi was an Italian patriot, who supported the movement to unify the divided country. *"Viva VERDI!"* became a rallying cry. This stood for "Viva **V**ittorio **E**mmanuele, **R**e **d'I**talia," or "Long live Victor Emmanuel, King of Italy."

Mozart

In Mozart's day, composers and other musicians made their livings by working for a wealthy patron. Mozart was perhaps the first to end up living as a freelancer. This was because he couldn't get along with his original patron, the Archbishop of Salzburg, Austria. Mozart ended up moving to Vienna.

About the Author:

Kathy Minicozzi was born on Long Island, New York and raised in the Yakima Valley, Washington State. She earned a Bachelor of Arts in Music from Eastern Washington University and a Master of Arts in Music from Washington State University. As an opera singer, she sang with the Regensburg Stadttheater in Regensburg, Germany, the Israel National Opera in Tel Aviv, Israel, the New York Grand Opera in New York City, Opera of the Hamptons on Long Island, New York, the Ambassadors of Opera and Concert Worldwide and other groups. Although she no longer auditions, she continues to sing as a church soloist and in an occasional concert or recital.

She has now taken up a second career as a humor writer, and has been a regular contributor to HumorOutcasts.com.

www.ingramcontent.com/pod-product-compliance
Lightning Source LLC
LaVergne TN
LVHW051247080426
835513LV00016B/1791
9780692553855